philosophizing

creating a world of ideas

ANDREW ALEXANDER

Kendall Hunt
publishing company

Cover and inside front and inside back cover images © Shutterstock, Inc.

Kendall Hunt
publishing company

www.kendallhunt.com
Send all inquiries to:
4050 Westmark Drive
Dubuque, IA 52004-1840

ISBN 978-0-7575-8140-3

Printed in the United States of America
10 9 8 7 6 5 4 3 2

To Hope, Andre, Joyce and Lance Alexander and my students in Philosophy.

Contents

chapter 1

Introduction

What is philosophy? How does one engage in philosophical thinking? The purpose of this book is to tackle both of these questions at once. Learning the art of philosophical thinking greatly enhances our appreciation of philosophy. Conversely, having a reasonable grasp of the history of philosophy increases our ability to philosophize in both theoretical and practical contexts. Thus, the questions regarding the nature of philosophy and the kind of thinking that this discipline involves are reciprocally related. Philosophizing illuminates philosophy. Philosophy inspires philosophizing.

MEANINGS

The nature of "philosophy" is frequently misunderstood due to its wide range of meanings. To do justice to this range of meanings, let us distinguish between four senses of this term: personal, institutional, professional, and intellectual. Philosophy, in its individual sense, deals with a personal type of meaning. In this sense, one might say that my philosophy of dating, for instance, is not to kiss passionately on a first date. Another example of this sense of the term is to say that my philosophy of child rearing is such and such. In the individual sense, a philosophy is a belief or set of beliefs that guides an individual's conduct. In its institutional sense, "philosophy" deals with beliefs that are shared by a social group. In this sense of the term, politics and religion provide significant contexts for an institutional philosophy. Thus, we sometimes hear people talking about "Democratic Philosophy," "Republican Philosophy," "Jewish Philosophy," "Islamic Philosophy," or "Christian Philosophy." Political platforms or religious creeds are frequently seen as summaries of institutional philosophies. In its professional sense, a philosophy may be seen as beliefs which should guide one's vocational conduct. Thus, the future teacher, for example, might be questioned about his or her "philosophy of education" on a job interview. In like manner, the future lawyer should be prepared to talk about his/her "philosophy of law" in order to secure a professional position. With respect to its intellectual sense, however, philosophy may be seen as an academic discipline. How is this academic discipline defined? A rough and ready definition is to claim that, in an intellectual sense, philosophy is "critical thinking about basic ideas." Unlike science and history, it does not deal primarily with factual data. Unlike religion, it does not deal primarily with ultimate values. It deals with the fundamental ideas by means of which we interpret our human experience. Thus, although facts and values are important, concepts are the keys to philosophical thought. But what makes a concept a possible object of philosophical concern? One distinguishing feature of a philosophical idea is that it deals with something controversial. Ideas that are simply derived by searching for factual data are not philosophical in nature. For example, if we were to ask about the number of people in this room, at this point in time, this obviously would not count as a philosophical question because a straightforward head count would give us the required fact. Philosophical ideas are not so "cut and dry," so to speak. But is it the case that all "slippery" or controversial ideas are to be counted as philosophical? This would not be true because some controversial ideas are not of central significance. To ask if scrambled eggs are better than boiled eggs, for instance, is not to engage in philosophical questioning insofar as this sort of question involves a simple question of taste. Philosophical issues must deal with central rather than trivial matters. Now suppose we have important conceptual questions like the following: Is kick-boxing a good sport? Is this question philosophical? To be sure, this is not simply a factual question, nor is it simply a matter of taste. Some people who are impressed with the variety of styles, as well as offensive and defensive strategies, might answer in the affirmative. On the other hand, others who are appalled by the degree of violence might not see anything good in this sport. Thus, it is clear that this is a controversial question. Furthermore, it is a fairly important question because, for one thing, the public's perception of this sport has significant financial consequences for various media outlets, as well as the people directly involved. Nevertheless, this type of question is not fully philosophical because it does not have very comprehensive implications. An embedded question, however, is fully philosophical. For example, let us examine this question: What does "good" mean? This question focuses on an idea that has a vast range of implications. After all, we refer to sports, jobs, persons, artworks, poems, books, movies, actions, etc., as being "good." Therefore this sort of question deals with a conceptual issue. It is, indeed, the kind of issue that philosophy, as an academic discipline, seeks to address.

MOTIVATIONS

Why should anyone want to study philosophy as an academic discipline? To ask this sort of question is to delve into the area of people's motivations. It is not unusual, at this point, to make a critical distinction between intrinsic motivation and extrinsic motivation. Whereas extrinsic motivation is caused by the perception of external rewards, intrinsic motivation is driven by reasons that are internal to the activity itself. For example, an intrinsic reason for studying physics or biology is to increase our understanding of the natural world. On the other hand, an extrinsic reason for studying these disciplines might involve preparing for a career in engineering or medicine, respectively. In like manner, an extrinsic reason for studying philosophy is to obtain the kind of general education that helps one to prepare for careers in law, education, religion, journalism, politics, etc. On the other hand, an intrinsic reason for studying philosophy is to search for wisdom. In fact, the literal meaning of the word "philosophy" is "the love of wisdom." The ancient Greeks thought of a philosopher as a person who demonstrated this love of wisdom by cultivating a broad devotion to learning. Even today, the final degree in many subjects is the Doctor of Philosophy – the Ph.D. We therefore use the term "philosophy" as an honorable designation even in other disciplines. To claim that only philosophy can lead one to wisdom would be an overstatement. It would be realistic, however, to claim that an intrinsic reason for studying philosophy is to pursue wisdom. This, indeed, would seem to be an ideal motivation for studying this academic subject.

AREAS

At this juncture, it would be appropriate to ask about the kinds of areas covered in this academic subject. Philosophy, like medicine, is a very vast field. In the case of medicine, we realize that some physicians are cardiologists, urologists, psychiatrists, etc. These represent only a few of the sub-fields of medicine. In like manner, some philosophers are metaphysicians, epistemologists, ethicists, political philosophers, logicians, aestheticians, philosophers of religion, etc. These practitioners represent some of the key sub-fields of philosophy.

Each domain of philosophy is identified by a central idea. Due to the controversial nature of this central concept, however, many competing theories have to be explored in order to do it justice. These theories constitute the various perspectives on the issues in question. Theories of "reality" are examined in the field of metaphysics. Theories of "knowledge" are explored in the area of epistemology. Theories of "art" are encountered in aesthetics. Theories of "society" are tackled in political philosophy. Theories of "morality" are examined in ethics and theories on "God" are revealed in the philosophy of religion.

Each philosophical area is entered by way of its distinctive critical questions. In metaphysics, some of the key questions are as follows: What is the nature of the ultimate reality? What is the relationship between "the mind" and "the body"? Is there a "free will" or an "immortal soul"? In epistemology, some of the essential questions are as follows: How do we know that we know? What are the best sources for knowledge? Is there any such thing as absolute certainty?

Does any pure objective truth exist? In political philosophy, some of the essential questions are as follows: What is the ideal form of government? What is the basis for justifying revolutions? What is real "freedom"? What is "justice"? In ethics, some of the main questions are as follows: What are essential virtues for a "Good Life"? What is the basis for distinguishing between "right" and "wrong"? In aesthetics, the main questions are as follows: What is the purpose of art? What is beauty? In philosophy of religion, some of the central questions are as follows: Is there a God? Are there good arguments for affirming, questioning, or denying God's existence? What is the proper relationship between faith and reason? These sorts of questions, as we mentioned earlier, deal with central, comprehensive, controversial, and conceptual issues. These constitute the critical questions which drive philosophical thought.

METHODS

The subject matter, or content, of philosophy is best understood with respect to the ways in which philosophers think. It is possible to know about philosophy without knowing how to philosophize. However, learning how to philosophize will increase our appreciation of philosophy. Philosophizing is an exciting, active process of thinking and philosophy is the product of this process.

Philosophical thinking is a form of critical thinking. There is a psychological, as well as a logical dimension that is involved in this sort of undertaking. With regard to the psychological aspect, certain assumptions about "knowledge" seem to be related to different stages of cognitive development during the college years. At the earliest stage, students tend to think of knowledge as "just facts." Many students, upon entering their college years, think of their various academic subjects as simply vast collections of facts. On this view, "facts" are always sharply distinguished from "opinions." The educated person, like the winners on popular television quiz shows, simply knows a lot of facts. The trouble with this view is that it soon disappears after the student encounters the problem of disagreements within disciplines. Different schools of thought, or perspectives, exist in most academic subjects and, sooner or later, most students will be troubled by disagreements between experts. In many cases, students will have the tendency to think that all so-called "knowledge," is merely opinion. At a higher level of intellectual sophistication, however, some students will wonder about the criteria, or standards of judgment, by means of which they could distinguish between different opinions. Thinking of ways to establish the reasonableness of one's view has certain merits. To be sure, it is better than the first stage of thought, wherein one assumes that the content of learning is always purely factual. Moreover, it also transcends the second stage, wherein one assumes that all knowledge is merely opinion. In contrast to the dogmatism of the first stage and the skepticism of the second, the third stage of thinking avoids both relatively naïve outlooks on knowledge and uses reason to guide us through the complex "grey" areas of inquiry. Exploring the criteria or standards for rational judgments, however, also involves detecting the values that area built into them. Examining the order of priority for our criteria, in the light of our values, leads us to adopting a responsible position. This ability to seek for responsible positions in grappling with difficult issues is one of the key goals of mature thinking. Philosophical thinking, it is hoped, should enable us to develop this habit as we learn consistently to philosophize.

DEVELOPMENTAL PSYCHOLOGICAL MODEL

The following diagram summarizes some of the shifts in college students' view of knowledge, from the standpoint of cognitive development.

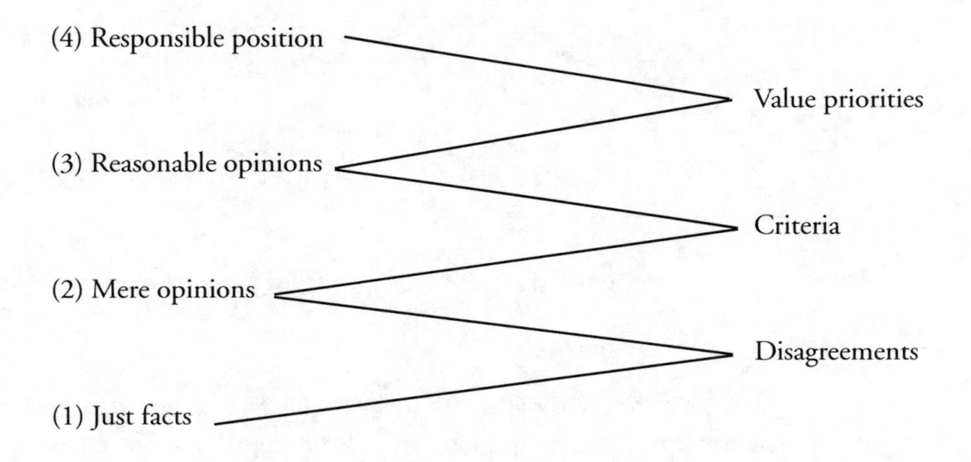

PHILOSOPHICAL MODEL

The question that now arises is how do philosophers think? This question is a very difficult one to answer insofar as there are many different kinds of philosophers who employ a variety of methods. Perhaps a more manageable question is to ask how we can develop a method for understanding philosophical thought and practicing it ourselves. But where do we begin?

The following diagram summarizes some of the key elements in philosophizing:

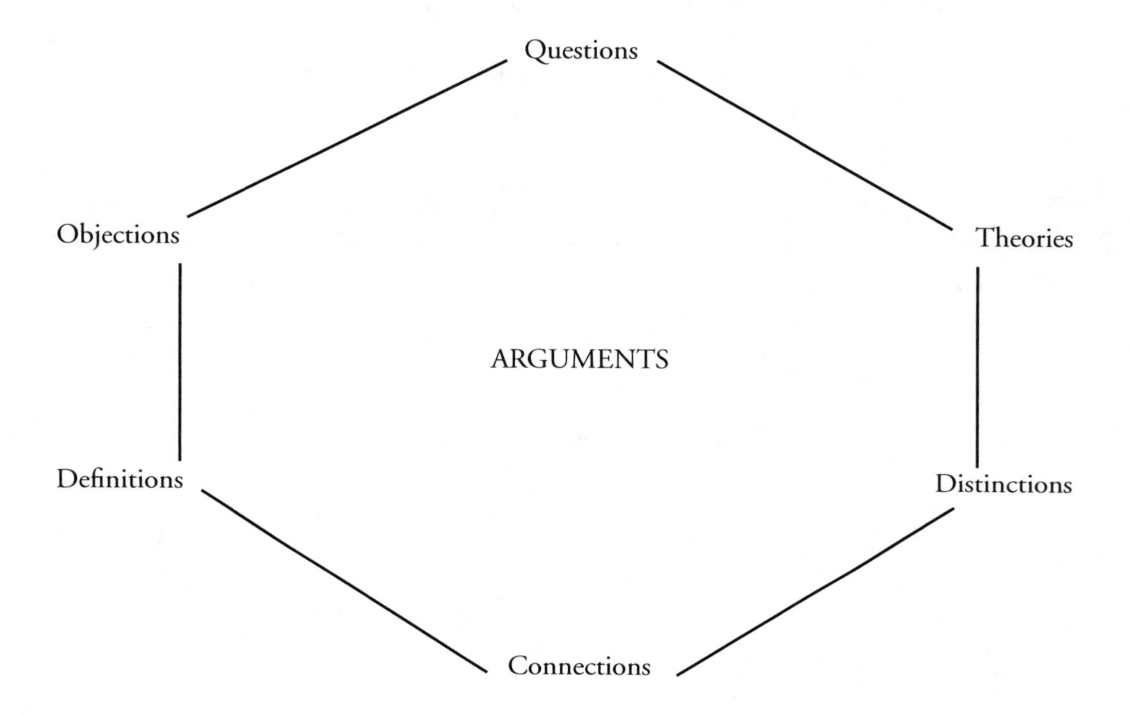

A good place to start is by noticing that philosophical thought begins by asking a relevant question. Philosophical problems are formulated by asking critical conceptual questions. Due to the controversial nature of a philosophical question, a variety of theories have to be explored. Various theories provide us with a range of perspectives from which to view the basic problem. Studying the history of philosophy expands our horizons and allows us to see key questions from many different angles. It thereby reduces the tendency to rely exclusively on conventional outlooks which, at times, produce a sort of "tunnel vision."

Questioning and examining theories, however, are not the only skills that are involved in philosophizing. A major ability that philosophers cultivate is the ability to define concepts. Many major ideas – "truth," "knowledge," "goodness," "freedom," "justice," "nature," "reality," "beauty," "God," etc. – turn on the ways in which philosophers try to define them. Practicing the art of defining major concepts is an extremely important skill to develop in learning to philosophize.

In addition to asking critical questions, exploring a wide range of theories, and defining comprehensive concepts; philosophers also make careful distinctions, examine systematic connections, raise constructive objections, and construct persuasive arguments. Raising or anticipating objections is an important skill insofar as it highlights deficiencies or inadequacies in a set of ideas. Finding counter examples or constructing counter arguments develops the basis for objecting to an idea. In order to support a position, philosophers engage in the process of answering objections by constructing arguments. Constructing persuasive arguments requires the formulation of carefully chosen supporting reasons (premises), which are designed to establish one's position.

So far we have been noting some of the elements that are involved in understanding philosophical methods of inquiry. But we have been doing this in a very general way. Thus, our comments might seem to be somewhat abstract. To provide some concrete specific illustrations of some of the major competencies at work in philosophical thinking, let us deal with a few examples involving defining concepts.

DEFINING CONCEPTS

An essential skill in philosophizing is defining concepts. It requires us to focus on the following elements: specific examples, necessary and sufficient generic criteria, and priorities. To get started, let us examine simple concepts now, and work our way up to the more complex philosophical ideas, in subsequent chapters. Simple concepts like "a widow" and "a good diamond ring," will help us start to develop some competence in defining ideas.

Let us take the first example by attempting to define the idea of a "widow." Philosophers would tackle this issue by asking the following prior question: What are the necessary and sufficient criteria for a person to be called a "widow"? The first necessary criterion would seem to be that the person must be female. This criterion emerges very easily as soon as one recognizes that it would not be logically possible for a "male" to be a widow. What if someone claimed that she met a very distinguished gentleman at a party last night, who happened to be a widow? We would immediately correct this error by reminding this person that a man might be a "widower," but never a "widow." Using a "male" as a negative example shows that being a "female" is a necessary criterion for being a "widow." But is this criterion sufficient? If it were sufficient, this would mean that all females are widows. Obviously we need to add additional criteria in order to avoid this absurdity. That is to say, for instance, we need to exclude "a life-long single female" from being considered as a "widow." This negative example would be excluded if we only included females who, at some point, were married, as possible candidates for being widows. A female had to have been married before she could be considered a widow.

But are these two criteria sufficient for capturing this concept? Once again we must continue our search. A "divorced female" is a female who "was married," but is not necessarily a "widow." This counterexample shows that another criterion is necessary – a "dead husband." Every widow has to have at least one dead husband or spouse. Now is it the case that we have all the necessary criteria to define this concept? Many people might be inclined to believe that we now have a sufficient amount of necessary features to define the idea of a widow. Nevertheless, after some reflection, a counterexample like a "remarried female" would force us to add to our list of criteria. Finally, we have arrived. We can no longer find a counterexample to refute our concept. Thus, it appears that we are justified in believing that the concept of "a widow" may be defined in the following manner – a female who was married, had at least one dead spouse and is not remarried. The following diagram reviews some of the key steps in setting forth a strict concept definition.

SPECIFIC (Negative) EXAMPLES	**GENERIC CRITERIA**	**NECESSITY**	**SUFFICIENCY**
male			
	(1) female	√	X
single female			
	(2) was married	√	X
divorced female			
	(3) dead spouse	√	X
remarried female			
	(4) not remarried	√	√

It is clear that this is a simple example of concept definition. This concept is obviously not a philosophical concept. Nevertheless, by illustrating the use of specific examples, and the search for necessary and sufficient generic criteria, this simple illustration can help us develop important skills in defining concepts.

To familiarize ourselves with another skill in concept definition, let us focus on the ways in which we sometimes need to prioritize our criteria. In the previous example, the priority system was simple insofar as it is very clear that the most basic criterion for being classified as a "widow" is being "female," while the most advanced one is "not remarried." How would we rank order our criteria in a more complex case involving personal preferences? Let us consider the following question: What is a "good diamond ring"?

In this "diamond ring" example, the generic criteria are not controversial, but the priority system is. Professionals in the field, all over the world, agree on "the 4 Cs": color, cut, clarity, and carats. If we were to fulfill all of these criteria in a perfect way, however, it would lead to "the fifth C," namely, cost. To avoid an unreasonable cost, it is necessary to make trade-offs. Now the critical question is the following: Which of the four criteria ought to be regarded as the primary one? A more general question may be formulated as follows: What is the most appropriate way to rank relevant criteria? The type of ring that a couple chooses is determined by what they consider to be important. After all, it is possible to get a very large cloudy ring or a very small shiny one. In the first case, carat weight is considered as the primary criterion. In the latter instance, the primacy of clarity is affirmed. To rank order all of the criteria, is to get a general set of ideas in order to make a reasonable judgment.

There are different ways in which to rank order the criteria for a "good diamond ring." For the sake of brevity, let us look at two possible priority systems:

Priority System I	VS	Priority System II
1. Carat		1. Clarity
2. Clarity		2. Color
3. Color		3. Carat
4. Cut		4. Cut

To make a rational choice in this case, one must explore personal preferences in the light of objective criteria. With respect to the objective criteria, there is a good deal of agreement. With regard to personal preferences, however, different priorities will lead to disagreements. To resolve disagreements, we should resort to rational arguments before making a significant choice about a specific diamond ring.

RAISING OBJECTIONS

In order to ensure that we have engaged in a valid exercise in concept definition, we must check our thinking. In defining concepts, three types of objections may be raised. The first type focuses on the question of "necessity." Is each criterion, or feature, necessary? In other words, could we have the concept even without a particular criterion? The second type of objection deals with the question of sufficiency. Is the set of criteria, taken as a whole, adequate or sufficient? In other words, do we need to add another criterion? In testing for necessity, we are seeking to subtract unnecessary criteria; but in testing for sufficiency, we are looking to add necessary features that are required by the concept. Finally, we must review the rank order of the criteria. What would happen to the concept if we changed the priority system for the essential features? For example, suppose our first criterion were switched with our third criterion, would that improve our definition of the concept? Checking the necessity, sufficiency, and priority of all the criteria are vital elements in the process of raising objections.

CONSTRUCTING ARGUMENTS

How would we engage in the process of constructing arguments? Arguments are frequently designed to answer objections. An argument is a set of supporting reasons which justify a position on an issue. Each supporting reason is called a premise. Finding premises for both priority systems, in the diamond ring example, would be an interesting exercise to consider before picking a ring. To illustrate the process of constructing arguments, however, an even more important dilemma could be considered.

The issue of abortion, for example, gives rise to many heated debates in popular culture as well as in moral philosophy. What would an argument look like on both sides of this hot topic? To do justice to this ethical issue, we would have to explore the pros and cons from many different ethical perspectives. At this point, however, in order to illustrate a simple pro argument and con argument, let us use the theory that an action is right if it could be based on a universal rational principle. According to this perspective, a clear set of opposing premises may arise in the following way:

PRO ARGUMENT

Premise 1: All persons have a right to choice.
Premise 2: Women have the right of choice.
Premise 3: Abortion expresses a woman's right of choice.
Conclusion: Therefore, abortion is right.

CON ARGUMENT

Premise 1: All persons have a right to life.
Premise 2: The fetus is a person.
Premise 3: The fetus has a right to life.
Conclusion: Therefore, abortion is wrong.

This example illustrates the idea that supporting reasons (premises) are used to create an argument. In this case, we sketched some of the main premises of arguments based on one perspective. Even one theory, it should be noted, can generate opposing arguments. Furthermore, to deal adequately with an issue, several perspectives need to be explored. Surveying various theories and grappling with the conflicting arguments that are generated by them, are some of the keys to philosophical thinking.

AVOIDING FALLACIES

Fallacies are "illegal procedures" that are used in raising objections or constructing arguments. There are many of them. Some of the major ones include the following – ad hominem, strawman, and red herring. The ad hominem fallacy is an attack against the person instead of the position. For example, if someone were to engage in "name calling" in order to deal with the proponent of an opposing view, this would be inappropriate. The strawman fallacy is an attempt to distort a position in order to make it easier to attack. For instance, a conservative might attribute a communist view to a liberal, or a liberal might attribute a fascist view to a conservative. These distortions would both be illegitimate. The red herring fallacy involves distracting someone from the issue at hand by introducing irrelevant considerations. For example, the attorney for a defendant accused of rape might try to prove that the victim was promiscuous, in order to distract the jury from the evidence and the arguments pointing to the crime. These types of fallacies are important to understand so as to detect invalid reasoning by oneself and others. Arguments, or objections, based on fallacies, needless to say, will lead us in the wrong direction.

MAKING DISTINCTIONS

Questions, leading to arguments, may sometimes be clarified by making careful distinctions between ideas. For example, in arguing about the nature of "philosophy," a good deal of clarity may be introduced by distinguishing between the personal, institutional, professional, and intellectual senses of the word. Philosophy, in its intellectual sense, as an academic subject, is not the same thing as philosophy in its personal sense, as an individual's set of beliefs. Although it is desirable to strive for a connection between the academic and the personal senses of the term, it is important to keep the distinction in mind.

Making distinctions and creating definitions frequently work hand in hand in clarifying concepts. To return to our main example, after distinguishing between the various senses of the term "philosophy," we can then define the features that characterize a philosophical question, in an academic sense. Academic philosophical questions, as we mentioned earlier, involve central, comprehensive, controversial, and conceptual issues. Personal and institutional philosophical questions, on the other hand, do not have to fulfill all of these criteria. Thus, these distinctions help to set the stage for an important definition.

Other important distinctions, which pave the way for a crucial definition, may be seen in the case of "love." According to Fromm's celebrated analysis of this subject, there are different basic kinds of love: brotherly love, romantic love, parental love, erotic love, self-love, and love of God. These distinctions capture important differences in the concept and set the stage for an inclusive idea, according to which "love" may be seen as embracing the following criteria: care, respect, responsibility, and knowledge of oneself and other(s). Again, we see that distinctions and definitions serve the cause of conceptual clarification.

Carving out a set of distinctions may also allow us to understand a system of relationships. Once again, at this stage of our discussion, let us explore a simple example to observe the ways in which making distinctions may lead us to discovering relational systems.

The structure of our government, for instance, may be understood by noting a few key distinctions. With respect to its branches, the key distinctions, reflecting our belief in the separation of powers, revolve around legislative, executive, and judicial powers. With respect to its levels, the distinctions refer to federal, state, and local levels. Putting these distinctions together gives us a simple framework to understand our entire political system. It may be represented in the following manner:

	Legislative	**Executive**	**Judicial**
Federal	FL	FE	FJ
State	SL	SE	SJ
Local	LL	LE	LJ

These nine categories in our matrix capture all of the logical possibilities and enable us to discern similarities and differences between every aspect of government. Our constitution, to be sure, allows each branch to object to the other branches' activities by the process of "checks and balances." Our matrix then serves to clarify this process.

Other relational systems are possible by making distinctions. A continuum, for instance, captures differences in degree. For example, with respect to degrees of competence, we may distinguish between a beginner and an expert. Regarding age, we may distinguish between young and old. Adding these distinctions together allows us to set forth a basic concept map in the following manner:

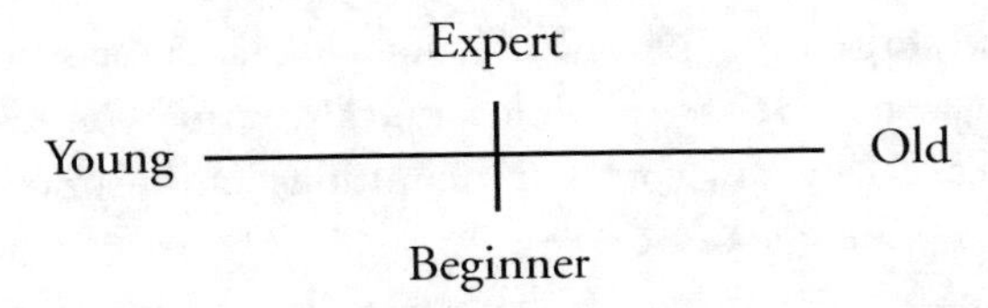

This concept map is constructed by using a horizontal continuum (age) combined with a vertical continuum (competence). Unlike the matrix model, where we encounter differences in kind, the continuum allows us to capture differences in degree. There is, after all, a range of differences in age. Thus, different kinds of distinctions require different types of relational systems to clarify the ideas in question.

Some distinctions only make sense when we see them in terms of a hierarchical structure. In the corporate world, for example, the CEO is at the top, different levels of management are in the middle, and entry-level workers are at the bottom of a hierarchy. In like manner, the Roman Catholic Church and the Army are organized in a hierarchical way. We may represent this structure in the following manner:

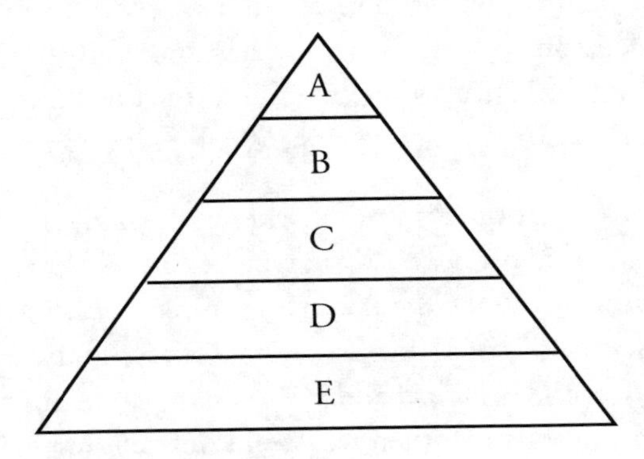

Making distinctions is an important job of a philosopher. It sets the stage for the discovery of differences and relationships between ideas, which can then be set forth in conceptual models. Using a continuum, a matrix, a hierarchy, or a full scale map, for example, allows us to represent the logical geography of central concepts. This is one of the goals of philosophic thought.

SUMMARIZING PHILOSOPHIZING

It might be tempting to search for a single formula to capture the sequence of all the skills that are involved in philosophical thinking. No such formula exists. To be sure, philosophizing begins by asking critical questions. Along the philosophical journey, philosophers explore various perspectives or theories, clarify concepts with definitions and distinctions, anticipate possible objections, construct arguments and create relational systems or conceptual frameworks. In the history of philosophy, the "super stars" have usually tried to connect all of their thoughts on the BIG QUESTIONS by constructing grand systems of coherent ideas. These systems of ideas are still alive today and are sometimes referred to as "schools of thought." In learning to philosophize, we seek to appreciate the analysis, as well as the synthesis, of major ideas. Practicing analysis is like looking through a microscope to examine the components of an idea. Practicing synthesis is like looking through a telescope to see "the big picture" – a coherent worldview in which all ideas are logically connected in a system. Philosophizing requires careful thought on the micro level (analysis) as well as the macro level (synthesis).

A FINANCIAL APPLICATION

After looking at the elements of philosophizing, let us explore a somewhat extensive example to see many of these elements at work. Since we have not yet been exposed to philosophical theories, let us tackle a very practical problem without the benefit of any theoretical resources. Let us begin by exploring the following question: What makes a financial portfolio a good one?

This question requires a definition. As in the "widow" example, let us examine the necessary and sufficient criteria for this concept. What types of assets do we need to create a "good portfolio"? To begin with, let us take the familiar example of cash in the bank. It would seem that this is necessary due to the need for "stability" (safety) and "liquidity" (accessibility). If we had very little safety for the principal and it turned out to be just about impossible to gain access to it in a short period of time, then we would not call our portfolio a good one. Some degree of "stability" and "liquidity" are essential. But are these features sufficient? Most of us would object to seeing these two criteria as being sufficient because of the lack of "income" involved. People who placed all of their assets in a checking account, for instance, would probably get zero, or very little income. This is the reason for including savings accounts, certificates of deposit (CDs) or bonds in a portfolio. By sacrificing some liquidity, CDs provide us with more income. Corporate bonds also increase the yield that we may receive. But is it necessary to have any income at all? When we consider that the purchasing power of money decreases over time, due to inflation, we realize that some amount of income is necessary to offset this. At this point, we may wonder if liquidity, stability, and income, taken together, are adequate features for our portfolio. Once again we must deny this claim to sufficiency by realizing that, over long periods of time, maximizing the resale value of assets usually increases the total return on our investments as compared to relying on a fixed rate of income. For this reason, equity-based investments, like real estate and stocks, are necessary. In the case of owning real estate, we sacrifice liquidity for growth in equity (resale value), and in the case of stocks, we trade-off stability for equity growth (appreciation). But is "equity growth" really necessary to have in a portfolio? During periods of declining markets, it may not seem to be. Nevertheless, over most 10 year periods, equity-based investments have outpaced fixed income investments and, consequently, have demonstrated their indispensability in a portfolio. Have we now accounted for all of the necessary features of a good portfolio? Some people might agree with this assessment until they remember the impact of taxes on their savings and investments. This forces us to add "tax advantage," using Individual Retirement Accounts, for example, as another necessary criterion for a good portfolio. Finally, we seem to have arrived at a very reasonable definition, insofar as it is very difficult to think of any further objections to our concept. Thus, we may say that a "good financial portfolio" needs to include the following generic criteria: liquidity, stability, income, appreciation (equity growth), and tax advantage.

To visualize some of the trade-offs that are represented by these criteria, the following diagram should serve our purpose:

INVESTMENT CRITERIA

EQUITY APPRECIATION

LIQUIDITY TAX ADVANTAGE INCOME

STABILITY

After defining our concept in terms of necessary and sufficient criteria, it is important to clarify this concept in terms of making some relevant distinctions. The most fundamental distinction to note, with regard to the variety of specific assets, is the difference between fixed income assets and equity assets. A fixed income asset, a bond for instance, is based on loaning money to a governmental entity or to a corporation in exchange for a stream of income. An equity asset, a stock for instance, is based on owning something. With regard to classifying assets, the key difference is loaning versus owning. Owning is frequently more rewarding than loaning, in the long term. In the short term, however, it can involve a higher level of risk. Different degrees of risk and reward are associated with specific investments in both categories. With regard to risk tolerance, the key distinction is between conservative investors and aggressive investors. Conservative investors prefer low risk - low return options. Aggressive investors prefer high risk - high return options. In the realm of fixed income investments, the distinctions in risk tolerance are reflected in the types of investment vehicles: long term versus short term, high yield versus high quality, and foreign versus domestic income (debt) instruments. Long term, high yield and foreign instruments tend to be much riskier than short term, high quality, domestic instruments, like Treasury Bills, for example. In the realm of stock investments, distinctions between the types of companies we could own are connected to different risk profiles. In general, small companies are riskier than large ones, growth stocks are riskier than value stocks, and foreign companies are riskier than domestic companies, for the most part. Conservative equity investors tend to like large domestic value-oriented stocks while aggressive investors might prefer small foreign growth-oriented stocks in their portfolios.

To visualize these risk-reward distinctions, the following conceptual map may be helpful:

DISTINCTIONS IN ASSETS; RISK – REWARD

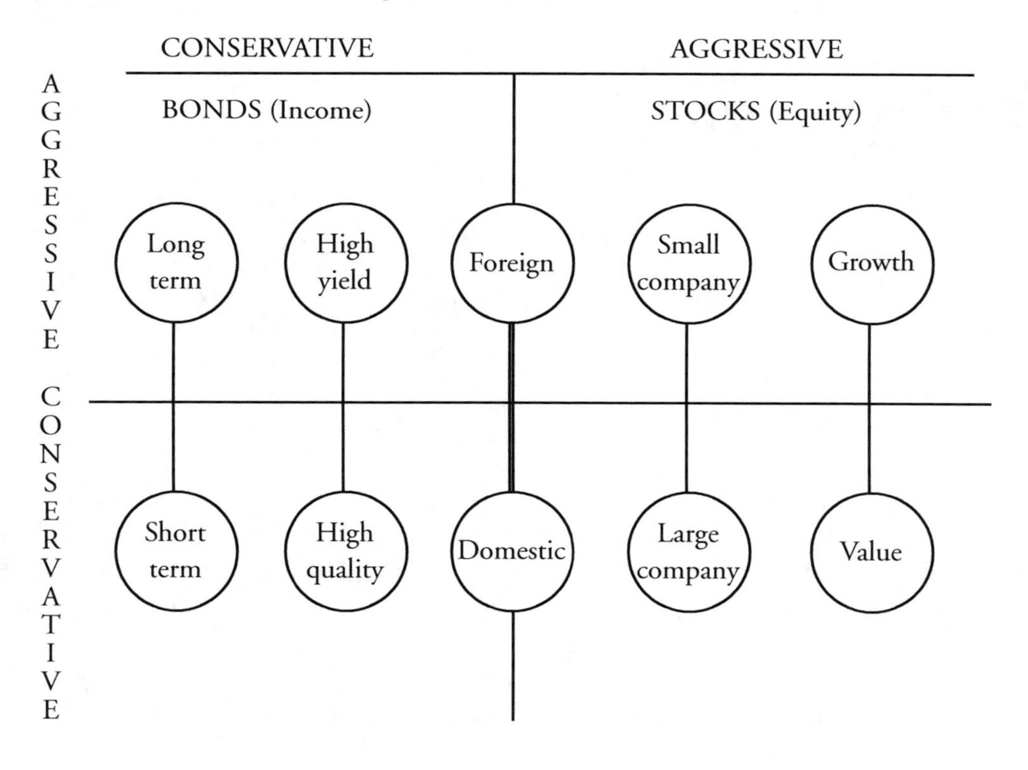

In this conceptual map of the financial world, representing diverse securities, the most aggressive option located in the northeastern section, is foreign small-growth companies. The most conservative option, located in the southwestern region, is short term high-quality domestic income securities, Treasury Bills, for example. Just about every type of security may be understood by finding its place in this conceptual map.

Now that we have distinguished between a variety of asset classes, it is necessary to make our priorities explicit. How should we rank our generic criteria and our specific assets? This is a very difficult question to answer in absolute terms. It is hard to say what all persons, at all times and in all places should do. Some logical guidelines, however, can be given. If we assume that every financial portfolio should include savings and investments, then the question becomes a bit easier. We can agree that the savings component should emphasize stability of the principal. But what should the investment component include? Taking into account such factors as time horizons and risk tolerance, we can set forth the following assertions: young aggressive investors should emphasize equity-based investments while old conservative investors should emphasize income-based investments. All investors should reserve a prominent place for tax-advantaged investments. All investors should have a diversified and balanced portfolio. For young people with a job, in their twenties, the investment component of their portfolios should stress the following features: tax advantage, equity growth (appreciation), liquidity, and income.

At least three major objections could be raised against this conception. First of all, we might object to the need for "tax advantage" by noting that it compromises our liquidity. Secondly, we might object to having any stock investments at all, due to the instability (volatility) of the stock market. Finally, we might accept the first two criteria but insist on placing them much lower in the priority system.

To respond to these objections, a few arguments may be set forth. First of all, with regard to "tax-advantaged" assets, we have to give up some liquidity (accessibility) to get a tax reduction. Gaining 15% to 28%, however, is worth it. Secondly, with respect to stock investment, we have to give up some stability in order to get maximum equity growth or appreciation. Gaining an average of 11%, long term, however, is worth it in order to stay ahead of inflation. Finally, we emphasize tax advantage and equity growth as our primary investment criteria because, taken together, both of these features can add 26% each year, over the long term, on average, to our portfolio. In short, these sacrifices are well worth it, most of the time.

After responding to these key objections, we are now in a position to articulate the implications of our concept. If a young person's portfolio has the features of stability, tax advantage, equity, liquidity, and income, then it is a good portfolio. Income is placed last. If the person has an adequate salary, it may not even be really necessary. If one of the first four criteria is missing, it is a mediocre portfolio. If two or more of the first four criteria are lacking, it is a low quality portfolio. All of the necessary criteria require trade-offs. No single investment has all of the necessary features. This is why a balanced portfolio of diverse asset classes is the essence of a "good portfolio."

The purpose of this extended financial example is to illustrate major features of philosophizing. We asked a fairly controversial conceptual question, searched for a definition in terms of necessary and sufficient generic criteria coupled with specific examples, made critical distinctions, generated a relational system, set forth a rank order for the criteria, anticipated objections and constructed arguments with supporting reasons (premises) to answer these objections. These philosophical skills may be used in a variety of practical and theoretical contexts. Whenever critical value judgments are called for, serious philosophical reflection is required. Whether the subject is money, morals or metaphysics, philosophizing leaves us with a valuable set of skills. This empowers us to make wise choices.

EXERCISES

Philosophizing requires practice. So far we have used a variety of examples to illustrate various facets of philosophizing. The "widow" example is used to demonstrate the need to define concepts with generic criteria and specific examples. The "diamond ring" example is used to illustrate the importance of finding a priority system, or a rank order, for the criteria. The "abortion" example is used to show the importance of arguments and counterarguments. The "investment portfolio" example is used to integrate all of the previously mentioned skills.

TWENTY TERRIFIC TOPICS

To sharpen your philosophical skills, practice the art of defining concepts by tackling this type of question: What makes an X "a good X"? Use the following examples for X:

(1) person (2) friend (3) spouse (4) job (5) career
(6) student (7) book (8) movie (9) car (10) bank
(11) hospital (12) restaurant (13) school (14) college (15) president
(16) pet (17) hobby (18) lawyer (19) doctor (20) writer

FORMAT

I DEFINING CONCEPTS

Identify the essential criteria, or features, of a key idea using examples and counterexamples.

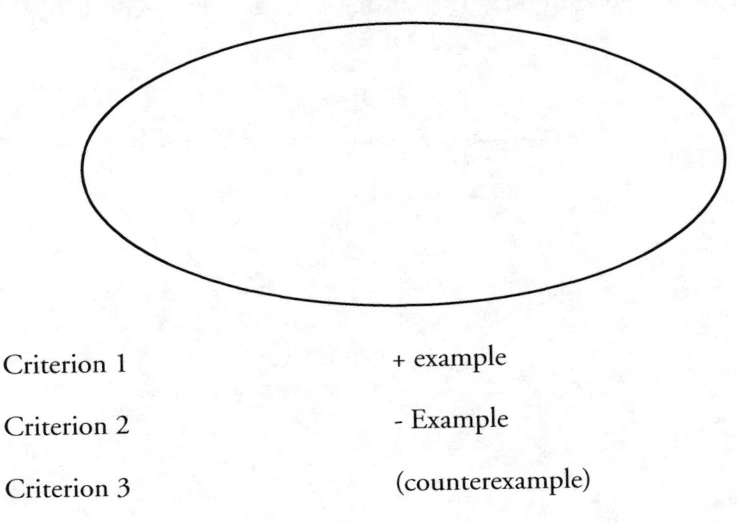

II ANTICIPATING OBJECTIONS

Question the necessity, sufficiency, and priority of the criteria:

(A) Necessity: Should we subtract an unnecessary feature?

(B) Sufficiency: Should we add another criterion?

(C) Priority: Should we change the line up of the criteria?

III CONSTRUCTING ARGUMENTS

(A) Provide good reasons for keeping or changing the set of criteria in the concept, in the light of the objections.

(B) Articulate the premises (supporting reasons) for the final argument.

(C) Explain the bases for distinguishing between a "good X," a "mediocre X," and a "low quality X."

If a group project is involved, the following roles, linked to essential skills, are required:

(1) Criteria Giver (2) Examples Finder (3) Rank Order Provider
(4) Objections Raiser (5) Argument Constructor (6) Writer.

In order to be successful, a good working relationship must exist between all members of the philosophical team.

REVIEW QUESTIONS

(1) Define three senses of the term, "philosophy."

(2) How is philosophy different from other academic disciplines?

(3) What are the basic ideas which professional philosophers seek to explore?

(4) What makes a question count as a philosophical question?

(5) How are the basic philosophical questions related to the fundamental areas of philosophy?

(6) Describe some of the essential elements of critical thinking in philosophy.

(7) Which practical concept is your favorite one to define?

(8) What are the necessary and sufficient criteria for defining your favorite concept?

chapter 2

Ethics

Ethics is a natural place to begin our journey in the exploration of philosophy. In one way or another, most people have thought about a question, at some point in time, which could be classified as being an ethical question. After all, is there anyone who has not wondered if a particular course of action would be morally right or wrong? Is there anyone who has not speculated about the nature of the Good Life for humankind? These kinds of questions seem "natural" enough for people to ask and it would indeed be surprising if we were to find someone who has never entertained any of these types of questions at any point in time. Merely asking these types of questions is certainly not sufficient to obtain a deep understanding of the complex set of issues that are connected with our moral beliefs. In order to gain a comprehensive understanding of the assumptions and implications of our moral beliefs, it is necessary to explore the various moral perspectives in the area of ethics.

QUESTIONS

Perhaps the most general questions that we can think about concerns the nature of the Good Life, and the basis for moral judgment. Accordingly, let us begin our exploration of ethical philosophy by asking the following questions: What are the necessary and sufficient virtues for a Good Life? What are the best sources for moral judgment?

PLATO'S IDEALISM

Plato (427-347 B.C.) made one of the earliest systematic attempts to answer these sorts of questions. According to Plato, beliefs about morality are related to beliefs about the nature of human personality, and these, in turn, are related to beliefs about the nature of ultimate reality.

The nature of ultimate reality is a question in the area of metaphysics. Nevertheless, to understand Plato's ethics, we must touch on his metaphysics since his beliefs about morality are logical extensions of his beliefs about reality. The ultimate reality, for Plato, is an ideal world wherein the pure forms of things reside. From this idealistic point of view, concrete particular things are not as real as the abstract universal concepts, which they exemplify. Actual specific chairs, for instance, illustrate the ideal generic idea of CHAIRNESS. Concrete specific circular things, like coins and pizzas, are representations of the abstract generic idea of CIRCULARITY. CHAIRNESS and CIRCULARITY are Forms which inhabit an ideal world. The highest forms are those noble ideals like TRUTH, BEAUTY and GOODNESS. An actual chair is good insofar as it conforms to the ideal "chairness." An actual person is good insofar as he or she represents the essential features of the ideal person.

What would the ideal person look like? To answer this question, it is important to notice Plato's assumptions regarding the nature of the human soul. According to Plato, there are three elements of the human personality – mind, spirit, and appetite. The mental aspect of the soul produces the intellectual virtue of wisdom. The spirited aspect of the soul gives rise to the virtue of the will, namely, courage. The instinctive appetites, in the soul, have to be held in check by the mind and the will so as to produce the virtue of temperance, or self control. Thus, the ideal person will possess the virtues of wisdom, courage, and temperance.

Are these virtues sufficient for describing the nature of the Good Life? Plato assumes that we should think of an overall virtue that links all of these virtues together. This most general of all virtues is justice. In terms of his priority system, since reason is the highest faculty of the soul, its associated virtue, wisdom, is the highest virtue. Since the will, or the spirited element is next in line, its associated virtue, courage, is the second highest virtue. Since the instinctive element is the lowest aspect of the personality, its associated virtue, temperance, is the least noteworthy of the major virtues. Justice, however, is the virtue of virtues.

This just person is wise, courageous, and temperate or self-controlled. This person's soul exhibits an inner harmony which leads to a sense of well-being and true, deep-seated happiness. In order to achieve this sense of well-being, however, reason must control the will and the rational will must control the appetites. In other words, "the head" must control "the heart" and together they must ensure that the unruly appetites, stemming from the natural impulses, are not given prominence in the conduct of life. Thus, the just person cultivates those virtues which ensure conformity to the ideal form of human personality.

ARISTOTLE'S NATURALISM

Aristotle (384-322 B.C.), Plato's most famous student, set forth a naturalistic conception of the Good Life. Whereas Plato believed that goodness was a pure, eternal, unchanging ideal form, Aristotle believed the goodness was always linked to natural function. A human being, like everything in nature, has a goal, or end, or purpose to fulfill. Goodness, in its different manifestations, consists in fulfilling one's function. In general, there are two types of goods or values. An intrinsic good is something that is good in itself. An instrumental good, on the other hand, is something that is good as a means to some other end.

Let us consider a few contemporary examples to illustrate Aristotle's point. A doctor, a basketball player, and a teacher all aim at achieving some goal or end or purpose. In the case of the doctor, the ultimate goal is to produce health. In the case of the basketball player, the final end is to win the game. In the case of the teacher, the ultimate purpose is to educate. Producing health, winning the game, and educating are, therefore, intrinsic values.

In order to reach these intrinsic values, however, we have to be aware of the instrumental values that lead to them. In order to produce health, the doctor might prescribe certain diets, tablets, therapies, or even surgery. To win the game, the basketball player might spend time dribbling, passing, and shooting. To produce education, the teacher might require the completion of homework, papers, projects, or tests. Whereas health is an intrinsic good, tablets, therapies, and surgery could be seen as instrumental goods. Whereas winning is an intrinsic good, dribbling, passing, and shooting could be viewed as instrumental goods. Whereas education is an intrinsic good, homework, papers, and tests could be seen as instrumental goods. Thus, instrumental goods are for the sake of intrinsic goods.

Intrinsic values serve as the justification for the related instrumental values. We could legitimately question choices regarding instrumental values. Questioning the intrinsic values, however, would seem to be silly, to say the least. After all, we could ask the doctor to justify the choice of tablets or surgery. We could ask the basketball player about the specific passes made in the game and we could question the teacher's choice of assignments. On the other hand, it would seem silly to question the doctor's commitment to producing health, the basketball player's commitment to winning, or the teacher's commitment to promoting education. All of the activities of the good doctor, the basketball player, and the good teacher aim at fulfilling the intrinsic ends, or goals, that define the very nature of these professions.

But what, in general, is the intrinsic good for human beings to aim at? An intrinsic good, we recall, is something that is good as an end and not simply as a means to an end. Therefore, even though we might pursue wealth, pleasure, or honor, these goods are not final or self-sufficient. We pursue them for the sake of happiness. Thus, happiness is the intrinsic good for humankind, according to Aristotle's point of view.

Now the question becomes the following: how do we achieve happiness? According to Aristotle's outlook, happiness is the fulfillment of our distinctive function. In the case of human beings, our distinctive function is to reason. Whereas other animals can do many of the same things humans can – move, eat, reproduce, etc. – only humans have the capacity to reason. This means that reason is our distinguishing feature. To be sure, humankind has basic biological needs that need to be met. But the distinctive human need is to reason. The good and happy person is the person who reasons consistently and well.

But how ought we to use our reason? Aristotle identifies two types of reason – theoretical reason and practical reason. Theoretical reason aims at contemplation of truth. Practical reason aims at solving problems. The major practical problem in seeking the Good Life, is to find the proper rational balance in life. Moral virtue, for Aristotle, is, generally speaking, a mean between two extremes. On the one hand, there is an extreme of excess (having too much of something). On the other hand, there is an extreme of deficiency (having too little of something). Moral virtue, for the most part, consists in finding the right balance between excess and deficiency.

A few examples of this principle of rational balance, or moderation, should serve to illustrate this idea. One of the clearest examples of finding THE GOLDEN MEAN between two extremes is the example of courage. Courage is THE GOLDEN MEAN between foolhardiness (an extreme of excess) and cowardice (an extreme of deficiency). Other examples of moral virtue would include temperance, friendliness and generosity. Temperance, for instance, is the proper balance between licentiousness (excessive regard for pleasure) and prudery (deficient regard for pleasure). Friendliness is THE GOLDEN MEAN between flattery (excessive giving of compliments) and quarrelsomeness (excessive giving of criticisms). Generosity is the proper balance between prodigality (excessive generosity) and stinginess (deficient generosity). The generous person, according to this principle, must not be too "loose" or too "tight" with money. From a moral point of view, we tend to admire people who are generous, temperate, friendly, and courageous. These people have honored the principle of rational balance in conducting their lives.

Now Aristotle also recognizes a few exceptions to this rule. The rule of thumb is that, in general, moral vices involve an excess or a deficiency of something. But not all moral vices follow this rule. Let us take the cases of adultery and murder as examples of exceptions. We would not advise recently married people not to have too many affairs or too few affairs and to strive for a moderate amount of extra-marital affairs. In like manner, we would not advise a new gun owner not to kill too many people or too few people, and to murder a moderate amount of people. These humorous examples illustrate the exceptions to the rule.

Nevertheless, Aristotle's basic moral principle, THE GOLDEN MEAN, is to live a life of rational balance. In order to do this, one has to practice the cultivation of the moral virtues as a matter of habit. The good and happy person develops the habits of rational contemplation and rational (moderate) actions. This fulfills our human function.

HEDONISM

The theory of hedonism was set forth by Aristippus (435-356 B.C.). It is simple. The Good Life is one in which the individual maximizes the quantity of pleasure that is experienced. A popular beer commercial, a few years ago, captured this sentiment with a statement to the effect that since we only live once, we should reach for all the pleasure we can get. This, in a nutshell, is the view of hedonism.

To be more precise, we should distinguish between psychological hedonism and ethical hedonism. Psychological hedonism is the idea that people's actions are always motivated, ultimately, by their desire for pleasure. On the other hand, ethical hedonism is the view that people ought to pursue pleasure since it is humankind's highest good. The latter view, to be sure, makes a much stronger, and much more controversial, assertion.

EPICUREANISM

The epicurean thinkers followed the philosophy of Epicurus of Athens (341-270 B.C.). According to this theory, the Good Life is the pleasant life. This sort of life is free from mental pain (anguish) and physical pain (disease). In order to achieve this freedom from pain, one has to focus on the type of desire that one seeks to fulfill.

The epicureans put forward a framework of distinctions in order to categorize the nature of human desires. Some desires, like the desire for food and drink, are natural and necessary. Other desires, like the desire for sexual gratification are natural but unnecessary, in the sense that the individual could survive without it. Moreover, some desires, like the desires for wealth and fame, are unnatural and unnecessary.

To enjoy the pleasant life, we must focus on fulfilling the natural and necessary desires. We have to take care of our basic necessities, but must be very careful about entertaining desires that are unnatural and unnecessary. The desires for wealth and fame, for examples, are extremely hard to satisfy and, consequently, may lead to mental pain. Desires in the second category, the desire for sexual gratification for instance, may be enjoyed if, and only if, a great deal of prudence is used so as not to cause long term physical and mental pain.

Epicureans promoted simple desires. Unlike the hedonists, they tried to refine the pleasure principle as the basis for the Good Life. They mentioned mental pleasures in contrast to material or sensual pleasures. Pleasures such as conversing with friends and appreciating the arts were seen as highly desirable in this account of moral theory.

STOICISM

Stoic philosophy started with Zeno (334-262 B.C.) and included the work of Epictetus (60-117 C.E.). Cicero, the famous Roman statesman and Marcus Aurelius, the notable Roman emperor, were prominent adherents of this school of thought.

The stoic theory of morality is closely connected with their theory of reality. For the stoic, all of the events in the universe follow Natural Law. This means that everything that happens, happens necessarily and whatever happens is for the best. The wise person, therefore, submits to the natural order of things and does not get upset if things do not live up to previous expectations.

Rational resignation is the proper attitude to take in the light of Natural Law. Let us look at a poignant example in order to illustrate this principle. Suppose our close relative got killed on the highway by a drunk driver. At the funeral, it is very likely that many relatives would be extremely upset emotionally. If we adopt a stoic attitude, however, we might respond by informing them that we believe "our relative's number came up," so to speak. In other words, even tragic events are, in some way, fated to happen and, in the long run, happen for the best.

Rational resignation may also come into play in a less dramatic case. Suppose we are saddened by the loss of a warm, romantic relationship that we hoped would be permanent. This could result in the sort of emotional upheaval that we associate with having "a broken heart." The stoic, to be sure, would not wallow in emotional self-pity but would think of this as a necessary event in the nature of things. A stoic would display indifference to this emotional trauma by affirming that his relationship was just not meant to be and/or that a better relationship will happen in the future. Indifference to pain, or the negative circumstances of life, is a major goal of this theory.

Perhaps the most appropriate metaphor for stoicism is the idea that life is a play written by a playwright. The playwright is Fate or God or Divine Providence. We are the actors. The length of the play and roles are determined by fate but the ways in which we play our roles are left up to us. That is to say, some things in life are beyond our control – our basic biological or financial inheritance, for examples. Other things in life, like our general attitudes and how we practice our professions, for examples, are within our control. The fundamental principle is that we should play our assigned role well, whether it is a major role, or a minor role, and cultivate attitudes that lead to contentment and serenity.

The stoics were also concerned about the social dimension of life. They believed that since we are all endowed with reason, the human race is one family. Consequently, this provided a basis for their emphasis on social service. This contrasted with the views of epicureans and hedonists who emphasized an individualistic pursuit of pleasure in their quest for the Good Life.

ST. AUGUSTINE

St. Augustine's theory of the Good Life is very heavily influenced by Plato's idealism and Christian theism. For Plato, Goodness is an eternal, unchanging, universal ideal form or IDEA, which is identical with Ultimate Reality. St. Augustine (354-430 C.E.) equates this reality with God. This means that all of reality, insofar as it is the creation of God, is essentially good.

But how are we to explain the existence of evil? Augustine makes a distinction between natural evil and moral evil. Like Plato, he thinks of natural evil as the absence (or privation) of good. Darkness, for instance, is the absence of light. A famine is the absence of food. An earthquake is the absence of stability in the ground. These examples illustrate the idea that natural evil does not exist as a reality in itself. It is dependent on the negation of something good. Good can exist without evil, but natural evil cannot exist without a lack of something good.

What about moral evil? Examples of moral evils would include actions such as murder, rape, and theft. For Plato, these sorts of actions may be explained as the results of "ignorance" of the good. Murderers, rapists, and thieves are "uneducated," in the moral sense of the term. For Augustine, moral evil is caused by misdirected love, or disorderly love. Everyone loves something. Due to our finite (or limited) nature, the individual is not complete in himself or herself and, therefore, seeks an object of love. These objects of love – the self, material objects, other persons, God – all offer some degree of satisfaction. Moral evil results from our misguided use of free will in loving other things more than God.

God alone offers infinite satisfaction, or ultimate happiness, according to St. Augustine. The other objects of love are limited in terms of the degree of satisfaction they are capable of providing. Expecting infinite blessedness from a finite object is a clear sign of misdirected love. Augustine believes that God made us for Himself and, consequently, our hearts are restless until they rest in God. The Good Life is the love of God. Moral virtues are manifestations of this sort of love.

ST. THOMAS AQUINAS

St. Augustine embraced Christian ideas with Platonic philosophy and St. Thomas Aquinas placed Christian doctrines in the lap of Aristotelian philosophy. Augustine and Aquinas, together with medieval Jewish and Islamic scholars, tried to connect philosophy with religion.

Like Aristotle, Aquinas (1225-1274) believed that the good for each type of thing is determined by the way in which it fulfills its function, or purpose, or goal. The goal for human beings is to attain happiness. Happiness has an eternal supernatural level as well as a temporal natural level. St. Paul is Aquinas' guide for the supernatural world and Aristotle is his guide to understanding the natural world.

The natural realm, for Aquinas, is governed by natural moral law. This law is understood by the use of practical reasoning which informs our moral conscience. Moral virtues require the use of right reason in developing good habits of mind and good actions. Intellectual and moral virtues include the following: wisdom, prudence, courage, temperance, and justice. Conversely, moral evils, for the most part, as any good Aristotelian would say, involve an extreme of deficiency or excess in the use of virtues. The proper habitual cultivation of moral virtues leads to happiness on earth.

Eternal happiness, however, requires a higher set of virtues. These virtues are spiritual in nature and come to us from a supernatural realm – God's divine grace. They are faith, hope, and love. Taken together, they lead us to our eternal happiness.

A foretaste of eternal happiness is possible in our earthly temporal existence. This would be the case if we focused on the highest Good – The Summum Bonum – the vision of God. Whereas material goods, pleasures, wealth, prestige, art, and power might be considered as instrumental goods, the contemplation of God is the intrinsic good for humankind. This ultimate good is also the basis for perfect happiness, which is only fully attainable in heaven wherein we will have an immediate apprehension of God, in his essence, as absolute truth.

HOBBES' EGOISM

Thomas Hobbes (1588-1679) set forth the idea that the physical or material world was the only real world. Like the hedonists and epicureans, he did not believe in an ideal or transcendental source of absolute values. Like Aristotle, he believed that all human activity is directed toward a natural end, or goal, or purpose. For Hobbes, however, the ultimate natural purpose, or objective, was self-preservation.

Moral values, therefore, are always related to our self-preservation. The things that we call "good," are things that are consistent with our "self-interest." This is the basic idea of egoism. For the egoist, the word, "good" refers to whatever the individual loves or desires. The word "evil," on the other hand, refers to whatever the individual hates or dislikes. Goods and evils ultimately refer to our desires or inclinations and aversions. We are always motivated to seek our self-interest. Thus, there is no such thing as "pure humanitarianism" or "pure altruism." All altruism is simply disguised egoism.

But is it the case that we always act out of selfish motivations? Let us consider a few examples and see if we can interpret them, consistently, in the manner of a Hobbesian egoist. Suppose we give money to a beggar on the street. The egoist would say that we did this in order to relieve our psychological distress at seeing the beggar's condition. Thus, this so-called example of altruism is really a form of egoism. Suppose a corporation contributes funds to help the victims of a hurricane. Once again, the Hobbesian egoist would see this humanitarian action as a form of corporate self-interest. The corporation might need a "tax write-off" and/or might simply want to secure for itself a favorable corporate image through good public relations. Thus, this is also a form of egoism. Suppose we devote our entire lives to feeding the poor as members of a philanthropic organization. This, too, could be given an egoistic interpretation. The egoist could appeal to psychological reasons in an effort to show that even altruistic actions are, in the final analysis, driven by self-interest.

HUME'S SENTIMENTALISM

In contrast to Hobbes' emphasis on self-interest, David Hume (1711-1776) put forward the view that the real basis for morality was a universal moral sentiment of benevolence. This feeling was the foundation for calling certain actions "right" or "wrong." An action is "right" if it is consistent with the universal sentiment of benevolence and "wrong" if it is inconsistent with this feeling.

Feeling, rather than reason, is the basis for morality. Reason, according to Hume, is restricted to two general purposes, namely, finding relationships between ideas and discovering matters of fact. Making judgments of moral value, however, requires us to appeal to emotion or sentiment in order to make sense of this domain of human experience.

Let us examine Hume's idea that reason plays a relatively limited role in making moral judgments. Reason, according to Hume, deals exclusively with "relations of ideas" or "matters of fact." The only relationships between ideas that we know about involve resemblance, contrariety, degree in quality, proportions in quantity and number. We have no knowledge of purely moral relations of ideas. An example like parricide could establish this point. Killing one's parent, we all agree, is wrong. A young tree which killed the tree that produced it, however, is not seen in the same moral light as Nero, for instance, who murdered his mother. We blame Nero but we do not blame the tree, even though, in both cases, the same concepts are rationally discerned. This is the case because our moral judgments go beyond concepts and involve feelings. What about reason's role in discovering "matters of fact"? Hume argues that morality could not simply be a matter of factual discoveries because we cannot derive an "ought" from an "is." There is a clear distinction between questions of value and questions of fact. If we examine a heinous crime, like murder for instance, we will never find any matter of fact which we could call vice. All we can discover are certain passions, motivations, and volitions, which elicit a strong sentiment of revulsion in all normal people. Moral sentiment, rather than reason, is the basis for moral evaluation. Reason alone cannot motivate us to be moral. Reason can help us to analyze the means or strategies to reach our ends or goals. Our ultimate purposes, however, are based on our sentiment or passions.

Moral sentiments allow us to distinguish between the vices and the virtues. For Hume, the virtues include justice, fidelity, generosity, veracity, tenderness, industry, discretion, perseverance, and friendship. These virtues inspire warm feelings of approval. On the other hand, the vices create strong feelings of disapproval. To employ some contemporary examples, we admire a boy scout helping an old lady to cross the road, but we have strong feelings of moral revulsion noticing a husky man punch his petite pregnant wife for burning his dinner. Thus, we rely on our moral sentiments in making specific moral evaluations as well as in determining our ultimate goals in life.

KANT'S RATIONALISM

In contrast to Hume, Immanuel Kant (1724-1804) maintained that reason plays a major role in the making of moral judgments. In contrast to Hobbes' view, he also insisted that morality is not based on self-interest but on the concept of duty.

Let us explore Kant's idea that duty is the basis for morality. In evaluating actions, from an ethical point of view, Kant argues that we should distinguish between those that are "from duty," those that are "according to duty," and those that are "against duty." Actions in the first category – "from duty" – are moral actions. Actions in the second category – "according to duty" – are, at best, prudential actions. Actions in the third category – "against duty" – are immoral actions.

To illustrate these three categories of actions, let us look at a specific hypothetical case – a despised mother-in-law. In the case of the despised mother-in-law, if her son-in-law allows her to die in a burning building, when he could have saved her life quite easily, we would see this as being immoral. Suppose the son-in-law whispers, "Burn witch, burn…" we would certainly classify this as an action "against duty", based on immoral self-interest. If the son-in-law saves her life, due to the expectation of a possible reward, we would see this as an action "according to duty." The son-in-law would be acting on prudential self-interest based on a possible psychological or economic reward. His actions would not be truly moral but merely prudential. If the son-in-law saves his despised mother-in-law, regardless of his inclination to be indifferent to her suffering, due to her frequent nagging in the past, we would say that he is acting "from duty". This kind of action, with no expectation of a reward, is truly moral.

Let us apply this moral category system to two more cases, in order to drive home the point. A drowning child and a car salesman may serve as examples for Kant's framework of moral distinctions. If a young lady, who could swim, refused to save a drowning three-year-old at seven in the morning because it might mess up her hair and, consequently, make her late for work, we would say that this is acting "against duty" based on self interest. If she saved the drowning child, based on expecting future babysitting jobs, then she is acting on prudential self-interest by acting "according to duty." If she saved the drowning child by realizing that this is the moral thing to do, then she is acting "from duty." In like manner, if a car salesman sells a car that he knows to be a "lemon" to a naïve client, at an extremely high price, we would say that he is acting "against duty" based on immoral self-interest. If he gives his knowledgeable client a fair price, along with his business cards, hoping for repeat business from good referrals, then he is acting "according to duty" based on prudential self-interest. On the other hand, if he gives a naïve client a fair price, realizing that this is the right thing to do, then he is acting "from duty". Thus, we have three examples illustrating the differences between acting "against duty," "according to duty," and "from duty."

But how do we know the basis for our moral duty? Kant, unlike Hume, held that a universal rational principle is at the foundation of all moral judgments. This universal rational principle is formulated in his famous Categorical Imperative, roughly, as follows: Act only on a principle that you can consistently will to be a universal law. This means that the actions which we consider moral are those that any rational moral agent, without contradiction, could will to be universal. Actions for which the underlying principle would fail the test of rational universality would fail the test morality, on this view. For instance, let us examine things that just about everyone would consider to be moral vices – murdering, cheating, and promise breaking. What would the underlying principle for each of these moral vices look like? In the first case, the principle might be as follows: Murder your associates if you disagree with them. In the second case, the principle might be: Cheat on tests that you did not study for. And in the third case, the principle might be: Break promises whenever you can obtain a clear advantage. Now the critical Kantian concept of rational universality would clearly rule out the adoption of these underlying principles. None of these possible principles could pass the tests of consistency and universality. If we all murdered our associates due to disagreements, eventually no one would be left alive. If we all cheated on tests we did not adequately study for, no college degree would be respected. If we all broke promises whenever it became possible to secure our advantage, no one would make agreements or contracts. These examples show us why certain actions would be immoral. Conversely, actions resulting from principles which we could will to be universal, display the sort of rational consistency that is the mark of morality. Without fear of contradiction, we could consistently will that all people acted charitably toward their associates, that all students displayed intellectual honesty on tests, and that all business or marital partners honored their promises. These types of actions would all be consistent with the Categorical Imperative, in its first formulation.

A second formulation of the Categorical Imperative sheds further light on Kant's moral theory. It may be summarized as follows: Treat persons as ends and never merely as means. To treat a person as an end is to affirm the intrinsic value of the person. To treat a person merely as a means, however, is to use the person simply for one's own ends. This, to Kant's mind, is the essence of immorality. The key to morality is to appreciate persons rather than to exploit them. The Categorical Imperative, which reflects our moral conscience, implies that there is an absolute unconditional command to show "respect for persons."

A categorical imperative is very different from a hypothetical imperative. The demand of a categorical imperative is absolute and unconditional, but the command of a hypothetical imperative is relative and conditional. In the former case, the demand is to act morally; but in the latter case, the demand is to act morally if it is profitable to do so. Whereas our prudential self-interest may lead us in this direction, our moral conscience, responding to a categorical command, shows us that we must respect persons in an absolute and unconditional sense. This is the fundamental universal rational basis for our sense of moral duty.

UTILITARIANISM

Utilitarianism is an ethical theory that was sponsored by Jeremy Bentham (1748-1832) and John Stuart Mill (1806-1873). The basic idea in this theory is frequently expressed by the following slogan: The Greatest Happiness for the Greatest Number. Bentham, the founding father of this school of thought in ethics, insisted that Nature has placed all of us under two masters – pleasure and pain. The goal of utilitarianism, therefore, is to maximize society's pleasure and minimize society's pain. For this reason, utilitarianism is sometimes referred to as "social hedonism." Unlike the hedonists in the Greco-Roman period, however, the focus is on society rather than the individual. Thus, the bottom line in this theory, so to speak, is not individual pleasure by society's pleasure.

Now the key concern for the utilitarian revolves around the ways in which we can adopt policies that maximize social pleasure. On this view, moral judgment is not based on subjective personal intuitions but on objective social calculations. The social consequences of our policies need to be carefully calculated. To accomplish this, a social hedonistic calculus is employed.

To calculate the consequences of any policy, a few criteria are needed. Some of the major criteria for evaluating personal or social policies include the following: certainty, intensity, immediacy, duration, and extent. With respect to certainty, the question is how sure is the social pleasure? With regard to intensity, the question is how strong is the social pleasure? With respect to immediacy, the question is how soon does the pleasure accrue to society? With regard to duration, the question is how long does the social pleasure last? With respect to extent, the question is how many people can be impacted by the pleasure?

Let us use a specific example to illustrate the general idea of this utilitarian calculation. A frequently discussed topic, in our country, deals with the question of whether or not it would be right to raise the minimum wage. To answer this question, from a utilitarian point of view, we would have to calculate the consequences of doing so. If it would certainly bring about an intense, immediate, long-lasting pleasure that would benefit the majority of people, then it would be good. On the other hand, if it would certainly result in an intense, immediate, long-lasting pain that created misery for the majority of people, then it would be bad. Admittedly, it would be difficult to make all of the necessary calculations. We would have to analyze a lot of data from economists, social psychologists, and sociologists. Data relating to economic stimulation, inflation, unemployment rates, workers' self esteem, family cohesion, etc., would have to be considered. This would be a complex task. Nevertheless, the way in which we resolve moral questions is clear. We calculate the consequences of different options based on the tendency to increase social pleasure and/or decrease social pain. If one course of action increases society's pleasure, then it is good. On the other hand, if one option increases society's misery, then it is bad. The degree of goodness is linked to the degree of pleasure.

But is it the case that goodness is always connected to social pleasure? Suppose we had to choose to join a "party group" or a "study group" on the weekends. With regard to criteria such as certainty, immediacy, and intensity, the "party group" experiences more pleasure than the "study group." Few people get an immediate, intense pleasure by studying. On the other hand, studying will probably result in pleasures that are longer lasting with the potential of impacting many people positively, especially if it has profound personal or professional implications. Adding up the score, however, based on these criteria, it would seem that partying is better than studying. In order to avoid this sort of objection, John Stuart Mill set forth an important distinction between quality of pleasure and quantity of pleasure. On this view, mental pleasures are higher quality pleasures than physical pleasures. Thus, based on this more refined version of utilitarianism, our moral responsibility is to maximize the quality and quantity of pleasure that society may experience, while minimizing society's pain.

Utilitarianism, as an ethical theory, contrasts sharply with the Kantian approach to morality. Whereas the Kantian focus is on intended universal principles, the utilitarian emphasis is on extended social consequences. Whereas Kantians think of duty as the goal of the moral life, utilitarians think of maximizing happiness as the purpose of morality.

EXISTENTIALISM

There are two major types of existentialists – religious existentialists and atheistic existentialists. All existentialists emphasize human freedom and responsibility. They see human beings as having unique, individual identities that must be held in the highest esteem. Since we will deal with the religious existentialists in the chapter on religion, let us explore the atheistic existentialists in this section.

NIETZSCHE

Friedrich Nietzsche (1844-1900) wanted "a revaluation of all values." He rejected the traditional Judeo-Christian moral values in favor of the values of an aristocratic Roman culture. His basic ethical outlook rests on the distinction between "slave morality" and "master morality." Whereas the slave thinks of values as objectively given by society, the master thinks of values as subjectively invented by the individual. The slave prizes social conformity but the master prizes individual creativity. The slave honors altruistic values but the master honors proud, egoistic values. The slave thinks in terms of good versus evil, while the master thinks in terms of noble versus contemptible. The slave's primary motivation is to end all suffering and to be comfortable. The master's prime motivation is to face challenges and to maximize power.

The "will to power" characterizes Nietzsche's "superman." Most people, however, are all too human and live lives of mediocrity. Preferring a comfortable life of social conformity – a herd-like existence – they readily give in to peer pressure and neglect the development of their individual potentialities. For Nietzsche, the exhilaration resulting from the maximum development of unique creative abilities is the noblest type of moral value.

SARTRE

John Paul Sartre (1905-1980) was possibly the most famous atheistic existentialist of the twentieth century. He defined the movement with the proposition that "existence precedes essence." To understand his outlook, we must focus on the philosophical distinction between "essence" and "existence."

The essence of something is its generic definition in terms of a set of logically necessary features. The existence of something, on the other hand, is its specific exemplification in terms of a contingent fact in the world. A unicorn has an essence but not an existence. We may define a unicorn as "a horse with one horn." To attempt to see a unicorn at the zoo, however, is to engage in a futile activity because, obviously, unicorns do not exist. A VCR (videocassette recorder), however, has an essence and an existence. We may define a VCR, roughly, as "a technological device that plays and records audio-visual materials." The VCR was created to fulfill this function. A good VCR is one that functions well. The existence of the VCR is contingent upon the level of technological development. The television had to exist before the VCR could exist and, at this point in time, the DVD is taking over. The VCR example is used to illustrate the idea that everything that exists, exists contingently. It need not exist and eventually will not exist. This applies to everything – dogs, cats, rats, etc. If there is a God, however, essence and existence would be connected. Unlike a VCR and a dog, God would have to have a necessary (non-contingent) existence. Human beings, to be sure, exist contingently. Without our particular parents, we would not exist, and we all will die eventually.

At this juncture, the big question is the following: What is the nature of our human essence? Several attempts have been made to answer this critical question. Some of the features that have been proposed in order to define our essential humanness include the following: rationality, spirituality, creativity, linguistic ability, tool-making capability, etc. Although there are differences of opinion concerning the features that constitute our distinctive human essence, most philosophers have assumed that there is, indeed, a human essence. This means that most philosophers have been essentialists. Existentialists, on the other hand, take the opposing view.

The central doctrine of existentialism is that there is no given human essence. In other words, there is no fixed universal human nature. Whereas a unicorn has an essence but no existence, a human being has an existence and is continually in the process of trying to create an essence or an identity.

Sartre's existentialism explored the human condition as it relates to this need for creating an authentic identity. He used dramatic terms to convey his ideas. These ideas revolve around the view that if there is no ready-made human nature, we are responsible for creating it. To be fully conscious of this radical freedom is to experience "anguish." For Sartre, "anguish" does not refer to a sad feeling after a tragic loss, let us say. Anguish is rather a privileged insight regarding one's absolute freedom to make crucial, life-defining choices. Moreover, these choices have to be made without the benefit of objective, universal moral guidelines, if there is no God to provide them. The absence of God gives rise to Sartre's idea of "abandonment." This, in turn, leads to his concept of "despair," in the sense that we have no assurance that there is a "future fix" for the world, so to speak, but we should be engaged in the process of fixing it by our responsible actions.

Taken together, Sartre's concepts of "anguish," "abandonment," and "despair" lead to a philosophy of action. Individual choices, commitments, and projects are signs of a continuous quest for self-definition. Self-creation, however, is not limited to an individual level but impacts humanity, as a whole. If we choose to get married, for instance, we commit humanity to the moral viability of this institution. If we choose to join a particular political party, we affirm the moral worth of that vision for society. Since our individual moral choices have universal implications, we are thus responsible for creating the human essence, which is always in the making.

DARWINIAN NATURALISM

Charles Darwin (1809-1882) along with his famous followers, Herbert Spencer (1820-1903) and T.H. Huxley (1825-1895) set forth the idea that our morality, like everything else, is a product of evolution. During the course of biological evolution, "social instincts" developed for the general good of the species.

Moral conscience, or the moral sense, developed to promote the survival of our species. Moral virtues are founded on social instincts rather than egoistic impulses. Altruistic instincts proved to be more useful in coping with the environment than selfish impulses. The fundamental humanitarian instinct is sympathy, which is the foundation for morality. Thus, instead of basing ethics on a transcendent source – God or Reason, for examples – Darwin and his followers based our moral ideas on our natural social instincts. This account of morality implies that even some nonhuman animals should be seen as moral agents. If one chimp gives a banana to another chimp, this act of generosity is a sign that some primates possess moral sentiments. Humans transmit moral views by social pressure and the cultivation of moral reasoning, leading to socially desirable judgments and habits. Nevertheless, there is continuity between human morality and the morality of other primates, on this Darwinian perspective.

CARE ETHICS

Care ethics was developed by Carol Gilligan, in her influential book, *In a Different Voice*, published in 1982. She put forward a female perspective in ethics in reaction to Lawrence Kohlberg's developmental theory. To understand her point of view, it is necessary to sketch the major features of Kohlberg's cognitive developmental theory, which she came to see as an expression of male bias.

According to Kohlberg's theory, there are six stages of moral development. The first two stages are on the preconventional level. The child on the first level acts morally out of fear of punishment and on the second level, the child behaves in a naïvely egoistic manner. The next two stages of development are on the conventional level. On the third level, the child conforms to stereotypical roles in order to be a "good boy" or a "good girl" and on the fourth level, the child submits to authority, as an end in itself. The final two stages of moral development are on the postconventional level. On the fifth level, the person has a legalistic contractual orientation and on the sixth level, the moral agent thinks in terms of universal principles of conscience based on logical consistency.

This developmental theory seemed to be quite reasonable and universally applicable. It seemed to be a great model for moral education. The moral educator, on this view, should use moral dilemmas to teach people how to engage in moral reasoning and improve their level of moral development. A problem developed, however. Males seemed to be more advanced than females in their level of moral reasoning.

Gilligan explains this phenomenon by saying that males and females think differently. In moral matters, at advanced levels, males think in terms of general abstract principles. Females, on the other hand, think in terms of specific concrete personal relationships. Males focus on the ethics of justice and impersonal duty. They emphasize logical principles, contracts or utilitarian calculations. Females, however, focus on affection, empathy, relationships, and friendships, in particular interpersonal situations – the essence of care ethics. This enrichment of moral theory came as a result of the need to supplement partial (male oriented) ethical perspectives.

METAETHICS

Whereas ethical theories seek to address questions such as the nature of the "Good Life" and the bases for moral judgment, metaethical theories deal with theories about ethical theories. Metaethics, therefore, is thinking about our ethical thinking. In metaethics, we explore the language and concepts that are embedded in ethics. Terms such as "good" and "right" coupled with questions regarding the existence of ethical objectivity, for examples, are examined.

What does "good" really mean? This metaethical question has a very interesting story behind it. Early in the twentieth century, "good" was seen as a simple, indefinable, non-natural property known through moral intuition. Later on, according to emotivism, "good" was viewed as an expression of personal feelings coupled with the desire for others to share those feelings. Reacting against emotivism, cognitivism held the view that "good" really means "worthy of approval." On the cognitivist view, an appeal is made to rationality and objectivity but on the emotivist view, ethics is reduced to the level of personal taste.

Is there real objectivity in ethics, comparable, perhaps, to the objectivity in the sciences? Should we think of ethics as simply personal taste? Emotivists, of course, think of ethics as feelings and argue that we cannot really argue about personal tastes because they are simply subjective preferences. Likewise, cultural relativists believe that ethics merely expresses the mores or social conventions of particular cultures. These outlooks, therefore, share a nonobjectivist perspective. Cognitivists, however, take the position that there are real moral facts. These moral realists believe that ethical propositions, like "generosity is good" and "cruelty is not right," are similar to scientific propositions like "water freezes at 32°F" and "Jupiter is a large planet in our solar system." On this view, ethics like science deals with statements which express objective truth. Science gives us objective universal descriptions and ethics gives us objective universal prescriptions.

The universal prescriptions of ethics set the stage for understanding the meaning of the term "right." Right refers to duty. A major practical problem is that, due to weakness of the will, we are sometimes inclined to neglect our duties. In addition to this type of problem, however, there is the problem of knowing what our duties are in certain contexts. Suppose we have to choose between repaying a loan and using the money to pay for an expensive surgery to save the life of a child. There are two universal prescriptions at issue – keeping promises and saving life. In this case, our duty to save life is a higher duty than our duty to repay loans. Metaethicists would call the first type of duty "an absolute duty" and the second type "a prima facie duty." When there is a conflict of duties, we have to determine which duty should override the other(s).

How do we know the nature of our duties? How can we distinguish between our absolute duties and our prima facie duties? Why should we even attempt to live a moral life, in the first place? To answer these sorts of questions, we should return to the history of ethics, analyze the key perspectives, and see which ones propose the most fruitful answers.

REVIEW QUESTIONS

It is important to learn both the content and the skills of philosophical investigations. Reading carefully allows us to learn the content or the substance of the discipline. The skills of philosophizing, however, require practice. To develop competence, practice the following skills by exploring the relevant theories, with questions of increasing difficulty. The following format gives a preview of the types of skills to practice:

1. identifying (simple, complex)
2. comparing (similarities)
3. contrasting (differences)
4. evaluating (positives, negatives)
5. rank ordering (prioritizing)
6. synthesizing (blending)
7. applying (defining, arguing)

Now let us tackle some philosophical problems.

I (A) SIMPLE IDENTIFICATION

Match each theory with one key description. Use one letter for each number.

Ethical Theories

1. Platonism
2. Aristotelianism
3. Epicureanism
4. Stoicism
5. Hedonism
6. Augustinianism
7. Thomism
8. Egoism
9. Sentimentalism
10. Kantianism
11. Utilitarianism
12. Existentialism
13. Darwinian Naturalism
14. Care Ethics

Descriptions

(A) Pleasantness, simple desires
(B) Love of God
(C) Self interest
(D) Individual's unique identity
(E) Individual's pleasure
(F) Reason (wisdom, courage, temperance)
(G) Reason, moderation, happiness
(H) Society's happiness
(I) Universal rational principle
(J) Universal feeling of benevolence
(K) Faith, hope, love and Aristotle's Virtues
L) Rational resignation, serenity, social service
(M) Concern for personal relationships
(N) Instinct of sympathy

I (B) COMPLEX IDENTIFICATION

(a) universal	(b) social	(c) individual
(d) absolute	(e) relative	(f) subjective
(g) duty	(h) happiness	(i) pleasure
	(j) fixed	(k) fluid
	(l) principles	(m) consequences
	(n) reason	(o) emotion

Using the contrasting ideas above, identify each of the theories in I(A) by using all of the letters that apply. For example, Kantianism (theory #10) deals with universal absolute duty from fixed principles of reason. Thus, the answer for 10 is: a d g j l n.

II COMPARING THEORIES

Explain the connections between the following:

(a) Plato & St. Augustine
(b) Aristotle & St. Thomas Aquinas
(c) Hedonism & Utilitarianism
(d) Stoicism & Kantianism
(e) Augustine & Aquinas
(f) Nietzsche & Sartre
(g) Hume & Darwin

III CONTRASTING THEORIES

Explain the distinctions between the following:

(a) Plato vs. Aristotle
(b) Epicureanism vs. Stoicism
(c) Hedonism vs. Thomism
(d) Hobbes vs. Hume
(e) Hume vs. Kant
(f) Utilitarianism vs. Existentialism
(g) Care Ethics vs. Kantianism

IV EVALUATING THEORIES

Explain the advantages and disadvantages of each of the 14 theories.

V RANK ORDERING THEORIES

After evaluating all of the 14 theories, justify your priority system. Pay special attention to your top four and your bottom three theories.

VI SYNTHESIZING THEORIES

Blend the theories that you believe will create a good recipe for the Good Life.

VII APPLYING THEORIES

(A) CONCEPT DEFINITION

Employing the criteria derived from your top four theories, and your own examples to illustrate each criterion, set forth your concept of The Good Life. Using ideas derived from your bottom three theories, raise objections to this concept. Justify your concept by answering the various objections.

(B) ARGUMENT CONSTRUCTION

Examine the following hot topics in ethics: capital punishment, world hunger, abortion, euthanasia (mercy killing), gay marriage, minimum wage, affirmative action, genetic engineering, stem cell research, animal rights, cloning, environmental ethics, drug legalization, or another topic of your choice.

Formulate a controversial question.

Using your four favorite theories, articulate the supporting reasons for the pro side. Generate counter arguments to support the con side. Justify your view by arguing for the most reasonable premises.

chapter 3
Political Philosophy

There is a close relationship between ethics and politics. Questions about the nature of the "Good Life" and questions about the criteria for a "Good Society" seem to be related in the minds of many philosophers. Ethical ideas seem to imply political views. Political views, in turn, seem to assume ethical concepts. Thus, the attempt to secure for humankind a good life in a good society is a concern of ethicists as well as political theorists.

QUESTIONS

There are a number of important questions in political philosophy: What is the nature of a "Good Society"? What is "freedom"? What is "justice"? What is the basis for the social order? Is civil disobedience ever justified? Some questions are mainly theoretical and focus on ways of analyzing key concepts. On the other hand, questions concerning civil disobedience and revolutions are also extremely practical. People have been willing to go to jail, or even to die for their political philosophy. On a less dramatic note, people have been willing to sacrifice a great deal of time and money to promote their vision of a "Good Society" by working for various political parties.

With respect to party affiliation, it seems that, in most elections, there is not much difference between the generations. Young people tend to vote like their parents. This encourages us to ask the following questions: Should our political beliefs be based on family traditions or philosophical reasons? Would it be better to catch our political beliefs the way we catch the measles or derive these beliefs from critical thinking? Most of us would pick the latter option. To explore this option adequately, however, we need to examine the major theories in the history of political philosophy.

PLATO

Plato made the first attempt to articulate a comprehensive political philosophy. His concepts of reality, morality, and society are inter-related. For Plato, the ultimate reality is the ideal form of Goodness. With regard to morality, the ideal person is wise, courageous, and temperate. Wisdom reflects the virtue of the intellectual component of the human personality. Courage reflects the virtue of the spirited (or volitional) aspect of the human personality, and temperance reflects the virtue of the appetitive part of the human personality. A just person is wise, courageous, and temperate, since these virtues reflect the ideal order for the soul.

The ideal order for society is similar to the ideal order for human personality. According to Plato's theory, each moral virtue, in the ideal personality, is embodied in a particular social class, in the ideal society. The virtue of wisdom is reflected in the elite ruling class – the philosopher-kings or guardians. The virtue of courage is reflected in the police and soldiers – the auxiliaries. The virtue of temperance is reflected in the farmers and craftsmen – the manual workers. In Plato's scheme of things, the ruling class, the guardians, are the legislators for the society but are not allowed to have a private family or private property, in order to avoid the link between power and self-interest. The auxiliary guardians are allowed to have weapons but are not supposed to have family or property. The manual workers, on the other hand, are permitted to have private families and private property but are not allowed to have any political power.

The social system is determined by the educational system. The class of guardians is made up of people with the most extensive education. The class of police and soldiers is composed of people with a moderate amount of education and training; while the class of manual workers is populated by people with the least amount of education. In the ideal state, all children, male and female, are given a broad education to develop their talents. The class to which each person is assigned is based on the degree of educational accomplishments. The social system is a meritocracy.

Plato's ideal political system is an "intellectual aristocracy": wherein wisdom is the dominant value. If the ruling class starts to focus on honor or social prestige, instead of wisdom, the society becomes a "timocracy." If money becomes the dominant value of the ruling class, this further degeneration from the ideal society is called a "plutocracy." An even lower type of system, based on the desire of the masses for an equal share of power and resources, is called democracy. The lowest form of government, based on the self-interest of a dictator, is called a tyranny, the ultimate political perversion.

A tyranny is a sick state. An intellectual aristocracy, on the other hand, is the healthiest form of government. For Plato, the state is a living organism, and a well-ordered state, ruled by wise philosopher -kings, rather than a selfish tyrant, is the only way for society to have a sense of well-being.

ARISTOTLE

Like Plato, Aristotle thought of the state as an organism that exists for a definite purpose. The state, according to Aristotle, is the association of persons formed with a view to the supreme moral good, namely, happiness. Once again, we notice a link between ethics and politics in the thought of Plato and Aristotle. Whereas Plato thinks of the ideal order of the state as having intrinsic moral value, Aristotle thinks of happiness as the intrinsic moral value in the state.

For Aristotle, man is a social or political animal. Nature has endowed human beings with the power of reasoned speech, in contrast to other animals, for this very purpose. Human beings are not fully human unless they inhabit a state. A person without a state is leading a relatively meaningless existence, like an isolated piece in the game of checkers. Politics is therefore natural and necessary for human fulfillment or happiness.

To achieve human fulfillment, "the parts" as well as "the whole" need to be considered. This leads us to Aristotle's basic criticism of the Platonic theory of society. Plato's focus on the unity of the state leads him to believe that a community of wives and children is the proper social arrangement for the ruling class. To Aristotle's mind, however, it is a mistake to focus excessively on unity. If a state is too unified, it will become like a household, and ultimately it will evolve into a one-man state. Moreover, this communal arrangement, for the ruling class, is contrary to nature. On a practical level, Aristotle observes, people care deeply about personal relationships rather than public matters. Thus, a community of wives and children would be psychologically unsound because it would destroy the natural forms of familial affection. A communal arrangement of property for the ruling class, as Plato recommends, is also unsound because "communism" breeds more quarrels than a system of private ownership of property. Since major parts of Plato's ideal society would be unhappy, the whole society could not be happy, in this scheme of things, according to Aristotle's analysis.

Is there one ultimately ideal state for all people, at all times, in all places? Unlike Plato, who insists on this idea, Aristotle is more flexible on this question. Relying on his observations of actual states, he thinks that there are different types of good or bad states. He classifies states in terms of how many people hold power – one, few, or many – and distinguishes between good and bad states. This allows him to set forth six possibilities: monarchy, aristocracy, polity, tyranny, oligarchy, and democracy. The following relational system should serve to clarify his concept:

POWER	GOOD	BAD
(1) ONE	MONARCHY	TYRANNY
(2) FEW	ARISTOCRACY	OLIGARCHY
(3) MANY	POLITY	DEMOCRACY

Aristotle believes that monarchy, aristocracy, and polity are good forms of government. On the other hand, tyranny, oligarchy, and democracy are bad forms of government. Each good type has its corresponding bad type. A monarchy could degenerate into a tyranny. An aristocracy could degenerate into an oligarchy and a polity could degenerate into a democracy. Monarchy, aristocracy, and polity are all acceptable forms of government. The particular type of good government that a state should exhibit depends on the specific situations and people involved.

For all people, at all times, however, there is a big difference between good and bad forms of government. In good forms of government, the rulers govern in the light of the common good of the citizens. In bad forms of government, the rulers are mainly concerned with their own private interests rather than the welfare of the citizens. For Aristotle, a citizen should be a person capable of ruling and being ruled. Thus, children, women, laborers, and slaves are excluded from citizenship because they could not benefit from political participation.

Aristotle's basis for these undemocratic sentiments is his observations of states at that point in time. With regard to slavery, for instance, he observes that slaves were usually large and strong. They are suited for slavery as others are suited for citizenship. He distinguishes between people who are slaves by nature and those who are slaves by military conquest. He disapproves of the latter form and approves of the former type of slavery. Plato, to be sure, based on his conception of the ideal state, disapproves of all types of slavery. Aristotle, on the other hand, relying on his natural observations, thought of some forms of slavery as natural and therefore justified. Unfortunately, according to his view, slaves could not be citizens.

The moral purpose of the state is the promotion of the good life for all citizens. A state's stability is a necessary means for this moral end. Thus precautions should be taken to avoid revolutions. In the case of a monarchy, the king should avoid despotic actions. In the case of an aristocracy, the powerful few should avoid catering exclusively to the wealthy class at the expense of the public. In the case of a polity, provisions should be made to ensure that all qualified citizens participate in the affairs of government. In all cases, the citizens must be educated in the spirit of their constitution to ensure a law-abiding and happy state.

IDEAL FORM OR NATURAL LAW?

One of the basic underlying questions in political philosophy has to do with the basis for government. Is government based on ideal forms, as Plato believed, or on natural functions, as Aristotle believed? The concept of natural law is implicit in Aristotle's thinking. To figure out what "ought" to be, Aristotle focused his attention on what "is" the case in his natural observations. Aristotle was clearly a naturalist, rather than an idealist. The first clear concept of natural law theory, however, came in stoic philosophy. For the stoics, the natural law is a principle of reason that rules the cosmos. Cicero, the famous Roman statesman, saw natural law as the eternal, unchanging, universal principle of right reason in agreement with Nature. Natural law is the only really valid law and should be respected by all nations at all times.

ST. AUGUSTINE

St. Augustine's political philosophy is based on the idea of natural law. Natural law, for him, is God's eternal law. Whereas the stoics saw natural law as the impersonal force of reason governing the cosmos, Augustine saw natural law as the divine reason and will of the personal Christian God ruling the universe. Temporal laws, made by a state, should be consistent with eternal principles of law, as revealed by God's natural law.

Augustine's concept of law implies that the church is superior to the state, since the former deals with the eternal realm while the latter deals with the temporal realm. The church is the domain of spiritual love. The state is the domain of coercive force. The ultimate purpose of the state is to prevent the wicked from hurting the public. The state therefore rightly has the power of the sword to curb the negative effects of human sinfulness.

ST. THOMAS AQUINAS

St. Thomas Aquinas had a more expansive view of the role of the state than St. Augustine. Whereas Augustine thought that the purpose of the state is to prevent the wicked from hurting the public, Aquinas thought that the ultimate role for the state is to serve the common good. Thus, Aquinas had a more expansive view of the purpose of government than Augustine. Like

Aristotle, Aquinas believed that man is a social animal. The state is not merely the result of the sinful nature of man. Even in a pure state of innocence, human beings would still need a state. The government's role is to sustain life, keep the peace, harmonize the pursuits of citizens and promote a high quality of life. This, in effect, is a more liberal view of government than Augustine's concept.

Aquinas' concept of law is also a very important aspect of his political philosophy. He distinguished between different types of law: eternal, divine, natural, and human. Eternal law is God's reason, which governs all things. Divine law is God's revelation through the scriptures. Natural law is God's law, which forms the basis of morality as understood by our conscience and practical reason. Human law is the set of social rules as formulated by society's legislators. In this scheme of things, human laws must conform to God's natural law.

This hierarchical concept of law has implications for the idea of civil disobedience. Civil disobedience, as practiced by such famous people as Thoreau, Gandhi, and King, for examples, is based on the view that human laws which violate moral laws should not be obeyed. Dr. King, for instance, justified his strategies for civil disobedience in the 1960s by appealing to this concept of natural law as a "higher law" than human laws. An unjust law is no law at all. According to King, laws which sanction racial discrimination violate God's natural moral law and, therefore, should not be obeyed. Thus, Aquinas' concept of law played a role in providing the conceptual grounds to justify civil disobedience.

NATURAL LAW OR SOCIAL CONTRACT?

Is natural law the best foundation for government? According to natural law theory, the social order is based on fixed given, universal principles in accord with nature and discovered by reason. With social contract theory, the basis for the social order is a social agreement, or covenant, or contract. Whereas the stoics, Augustine and Aquinas believed in natural law as the foundation for society, the early modern philosophers (Hobbes, Locke, and Rousseau) introduced the idea that a social contract is the proper basis for the social order.

HOBBES

Thomas Hobbes was the founder of social contract theory in the early modern period. He had a very different concept of natural law. For Hobbes, the natural laws are the practical principles of prudence that serve the individual's self-interest. The first natural law is to seek peace, if possible, or use force in self-defense, if necessary. This is the law of self-preservation.

The second law is to allow yourself as much liberty as you allow others. The third law is that people must fulfill their agreements.

People must be forced to keep their social agreements, since this is the basis for justice. How will this be guaranteed? Hobbes insisted that people would have to transfer their rights and power to a strong, central sovereign power that could make sure that social contracts are honored. He called this sovereign power, the Leviathan. (The term means sea monster.) To transfer their rights and power to the Leviathan is to create a social contract.

What would happen if people failed to create a social contract? Hobbes' idea is that they would be stuck in "a state of nature," without the benefits of government to create a "civil society." Life in this "state of nature" would be "solitary, poor, nasty, brutish, and short". Strife, chaos, and deception would reign. Murder, rape, and theft would be standard operating procedures in the pursuit of individual self-interest. Fortunately, people have brains. This explains why they would form a social contract in order to leave "the state of nature" and create a "civil society" wherein some degree of order, peace, safety, and civilization could flourish.

The social contract is a contract between the subjects of the Leviathan. It is an absolute, irrevocable, and unconditional transfer of rights and power to the Leviathan. It is not a contract between the subjects and the Leviathan. The Leviathan is given all power to create and enforce laws. The Leviathan's laws for civil society create the conditions for culture, education, industry, and commerce to grow. The Leviathan itself is above the law but has the duty to punish those who break the law.

Hobbes' concept of the Leviathan shows his intense desire for order. This craving for social order leads him to favor authoritarian government. He was the first person to use social contract theory as the basis for government. Later contractarian theorists would lay the theoretical foundation for democratic government.

LOCKE

John Locke is the father of modern democratic theory. Like Hobbes, he starts his political reflections by contrasting "the state of nature" with "the civil society." His assumptions about "the state of nature," however, are very different from Hobbes' views. Hobbes was very pessimistic about "the state of nature" because, in his view, people driven by their self-interest would live in a state of "war of all against all." To avoid this anarchy, an authoritarian government is necessary, according to Hobbes. Locke, however, had more optimistic assumptions about "the state of nature." He sees it as a state in which all people would be free, equal, and independent. Moreover, reason would teach them to respect the natural rights of others – life, liberty, health, and property. To safeguard these natural rights, governments are instituted based on the consent of the governed.

Locke's concept of this social contract, which justifies the existence of government in the first place, is not the same as Hobbes' concept and has very different implications. For Hobbes, people in the state of nature would transfer their rights to the government. For Locke, people in the state of nature would entrust their God-given rights to the government. Government is thus, a trustee and not a leviathan, for Locke. It exists to protect basic human rights.

A good government has certain distinctive features. In a fair manner, it formulates and enforces laws for the good of the people. It separates power. That is to say, its legislative branch is different from its executive branch. The monarch, for instance, does not have the power to make laws. This power is reserved for the legislative branch, which reflects the sovereignty of the people. In a good government, the power to make laws cannot be transferred to the king or the executive. Moreover, a good government refrains from raising taxes without the consent of the people.

What if the government is a bad government? Locke held the view that a government could and should be changed under certain conditions. Since government is based on the "consent of the governed," the natural rights of the people rather than the "divine right of kings," is the primary consideration. All governments make mistakes. If there is a "long train of abuses," however, then this shows that there is a deliberate and systematic attempt to undermine the basic natural human rights. Whereas people will tolerate mistakes due to human imperfections, they have the right and the duty to revolt against tyrannical government. A tyranny, in Locke's view, contradicts the fundamental reason for having government. It is an immoral type of government because it undermines the rights that people have, even in a state of nature. Thus, revolutions can be justified.

Locke's theory justified the English "Glorious Revolution" of 1688. Almost a century later, it provided the philosophical basis for the American Revolution in 1776. Jefferson, the founding father who played the leading role in writing "The Declaration of Independence", used Locke's social contract theory to justify America's desire for independence. According to Jefferson, the basic natural rights – life, liberty, and the pursuit of happiness – were systematically undermined by a tyrannical British government. Thus, the American Revolution was another context in which the implications of social contract theory were felt.

ROUSSEAU

Jean Jacques Rousseau (1712-1778), like Locke, used social contract theory to justify the right to revolt. The leaders of the French Revolution (1789) were greatly impacted by Rousseau's political philosophy. The ideals of the French Revolution – liberty, equality, and fraternity – were all eloquently expressed in the writings of Rousseau. The French Revolution's leaders, in effect, were disciples of Rousseau who translated his theory into very violent actions.

Like Hobbes and Locke, Rousseau explored the idea of life without government, in a state of nature. Especially during the early phase of his political thinking, Rousseau believed that the state of nature was ideal. The primitive state was a noble state of humankind. Contrary to Hobbes' view, the state of nature was more like paradise than like a jungle. It was a state of natural freedom and equality. The first person to claim that a part of nature was his "private property", however, was the true founder of civil society. Slavery, exploitation, and misery came as a result of this unfortunate development. We would have been better off not to listen to this imposter and to remain in the state of nature, according to Rousseau's early view.

Later on, however, Rousseau changed his mind. He came to believe that a civil society would be a good idea if it were based on "the general will" of the people. Based on a fair social contract, people would trade their natural liberty for civil liberty. They would prefer to live by the principle that "law makes right" rather than the principle that "might makes right." The desire for civil liberty and the rule of law gives rise to the need for a social contract.

According to Rousseau, citizens have the right to terminate the social contract, at any time. They have the right to fire the king, for instance, if he ruled badly. This, of course, means that Rousseau, like Locke, provided a justification for revolution.

Rousseau's emphasis on the need to think in terms of "the general will" in all political matters, however, seems to establish a basis for totalitarianism. Rousseau believed that "the community" was a living entity, over and above the individuals who comprised it. Citizens, therefore, are always obligated to obey "the general will" of the people and may be punished by the death penalty for acts of civil disobedience. Furthermore, since "the general will" cannot be divided, there cannot be a "division of powers" in the state. This, to be sure, is quite different from Locke's idea. Government officials, in Rousseau's outlook, are seen as the people's deputies rather than their representatives. This means that Rousseau placed all power in the hands of the people, as reflected in "the general will." Thus, Rousseau's social contract theory reinforced the ideals of democracy and, possibly, foreshadowed the emergence of modern totalitarian government.

ILL

John Stuart Mill, (1806-1873), like Locke and Rousseau, spent a good deal of time on the idea of liberty. As a utilitarian in ethics, he also believed in the greatest happiness for the greatest number of people. In contrast to Rousseau, however, he did not see the society as a living entity, as distinct from the individuals in it. In contrast to Locke, he did not believe in God-given natural rights. His basic assumption, as a classic liberal, is that the general happiness means that individuals should enjoy as much personal freedom as possible, as long as the freedom of others is not compromised. For Mill, personal liberty is essential for the happiness of society and should not be restrained, as long as others are not harmed.

Personal liberties all stem from the freedom of thought. The freedom of speech, the press, assembly, religion, taste, pursuits, etc., all revolve around intellectual freedom. Mill offered an extensive set of arguments in order to justify his fundamental belief in the freedom of thought. The following chart should serve to summarize his view:

CASES	ACCEPTED MAJORITY OPINION	SILENCED MINORITY OPINION	REASONS FOR FREE THOUGHT
1	False	True	Discover Truth
2	False - True	True - False	Blend or Synthesize Truth
3	True	False	Understand Truth

For Mill, intellectual freedom is always good for society. Societies tend to have accepted majority opinions and silenced minority opinions on many subjects. Accepted opinions are usually thought of as true, good, and noble by the majority. Minority opinions are frequently silenced because they are seen as false, evil, or socially undesirable by the majority. Mill argued against silencing unpopular opinions. In the first case, the silenced opinion might be true. Allowing it to be expressed, therefore, might allow us to discover truth. In the second case, the silenced opinion might contain important elements of truth and falsehood while the majority opinion might contain a different mixture of falsehood and truth. In this case, if both opinions are expressed, society could be able to combine the elements of truth in both opposing views and end up with a new blend or synthesis of "the whole truth" on a particular topic. But what about the third possibility? What if the minority opinion is really false? Would we not be better off silencing it forever? Mill argued that, in this third case, even false opinions should be allowed to be expressed. If the majority opinion is really true, the facts and arguments which establish its truth would be much better understood if this opinion had to compete with a false opinion. A full understanding of truth is only possible when all ideas on a topic are expressed. It is possible to know the truth merely as a dogma, an unquestioned belief, without really understanding the reasons which justify it. This is why, in the interest of understanding the basis for truth, even false beliefs should be allowed expression. In all cases, intellectual freedom leads to the advancement of truth in society. An open society, that allows a wide variety of philosophical, moral, religious, political, aesthetic, and scientific opinions to be expressed, is a society that provides the best environment for continuous progress.

For Mill, the form of government which is best suited to promote intellectual freedom, happiness, and progress is a representative democracy. To protect the interests of all people, however, and avoid "the tyranny of the majority," policies such as mandatory education, proportional representation, and universal suffrage are necessary. Maximizing the happiness of all members of society and promoting individual freedom are the major values in Mill's philosophy. The world should be reformed in the light of these values, according to liberalism.

ARX

Karl Marx (1818-1883), favored revolution rather than reformation. His theory, communism, advocates the common ownership of the means of production – land and factories. The technical term for communism is "dialectical materialism." Marxism or dialectical materialism is a form of economic determinism.

Marx's interpretation of history is based on the idea that socio-economic forces determine historical changes. The following chart should serve to illustrate Marx's dialectical view of history:

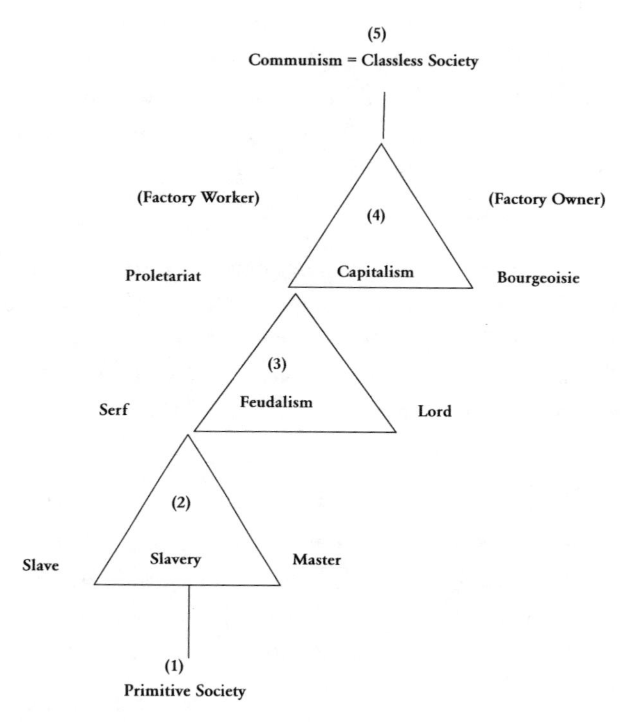

In the first phase of history, we find a primitive society with a communal socio-economic structure. In the second phase, we encounter slavery with its associated class conflict – masters versus slaves. In the third phase, we discover feudalism with its specific class conflict – lords versus serfs. In the fourth phase, we notice the development of capitalism with its distinctive class conflict – bourgeoisie (factory owners) versus proletariat (factory workers). In the fifth and final phase, history will be consummated by the development of communism – a classless society. This fulfillment of history means the end of all class conflicts.

History moves in a dialectical manner. An initial state of affairs (the thesis) develops to a point where it produces its own negation (the anti-thesis). The thesis and the anti-thesis remain in tension with each other until another social condition emerges which surpasses each and resolves the contradiction (the synthesis). Conflicts or class struggles in history are inevitable. History moves toward higher and higher stages in order to maximize productive capacities. Each phase of history is more productive than an earlier phase but is burdened by its own internal contradictions and problems.

Marx focused his attention on the problems of capitalism. In a capitalist society, the means of production – large factories, for example, are owned by relatively few people. Factory owners control society. In order to survive, factory workers must sell their labor to the factory owners. The price of labor, in this system, is set by the law of supply and demand. A large supply of workers, therefore, drives down wages to a subsistence level. It is in the economic interest of the factory owners to have children in the labor force, for instance, because this decreases the price of labor. Forcing workers to work very long hours, often in unsanitary conditions, further drives down the costs of doing business. Since the product of labor is a lot more valuable than the cost of labor, the factory owners (the bourgeoisie) get the difference – "the surplus value," to use Marx's phrase.

Economic exploitation is only one of the problems in the system of capitalism. In this system, specialization, which increases profits for the factory owners, often leads to dehumanization. Workers frequently must perform increasingly specialized functions alongside machines, in order to maximize productivity. The worker is, in effect, a part of the machinery and feels alienated from the products that are mass-produced. To increase profits, capitalists frequently produce too many goods for the market to handle. This leads to "boom and bust" cycles with workers being forced into unemployment during periods of recession. Economic forces conspire against the working class, according to Marx's theory, in a capitalist system.

Economic interests also determine the ideas in a society, in any period of history. The dominant ideas reflect the economic interests of the ruling class in any specific era. The economic substructure (the forces and relations of production) determines the conceptual superstructure (the art, literature, philosophy, religion, morality, and law) of society. Artistic images reflect the consciousness of the ruling class. Philosophical concepts serve the interests of the dominant class. Religious values sanction the economic interests of the ruling class. Moral norms and legal forms protect the interests of the dominant class. In a capitalist society, all the aspects of culture reflect the economic interests of the factory owners.

Marx's economic determinism means that economics determines the political, legal, and cultural aspects of every society. The change from private to public ownership of land and factories implies that a communist revolution will produce a cultural revolution. A classless society, the essence of communism, will engender a socialist consciousness and culture. Economic exploitation and personal alienation will be over and humankind will enjoy a socialist way of life, as the crowning achievement of revolutionary activity coupled with historical necessity. This, in short, is Marx's perspective.

MUSSOLINI

Although Mussolini is not considered to be a philosopher, his ideology, namely fascism, had a great impact on the twentieth century. It was the official view in Italy just before and during World War II. Hitler's Nazism shared many of its key beliefs. Whereas communism is classified as left wing totalitarianism, fascism is classified as right wing totalitarianism. All forms of totalitarianism assume that one particular ideology should govern the totality of life.

Mussolini's fascism assumes that the state is an organic whole. It is a living entity which requires spiritual unity. Every aspect of life – politics, economics, education, religion, mass media, entertainment, etc., – should serve the interests of the state. Only one political party is allowed because the state should be undivided. Different economic classes may exist as long as the spiritual unity of the state is maintained. Religious, educational, and media organizations are not allowed to criticize the state or its leaders. The leader, for instance, is the incarnation of the state. Mussolini, for example, thought of himself as the embodiment of the spirit of Italy. The leader is assisted by a ruling elite. All individuals exist to serve the state and any individual who fails to do this, is living a meaningless existence.

Fascists believe that growth is the sign of a healthy state. Healthy states grow and diseased states do not. War allows the state to grow. Thus, according to fascist ideology, war is good and imperialism is justified.

RAWLS

John Rawls (1921-2002) set forth a recent version of liberalism based on a more abstract account of social contract theory. His fundamental concept of justice is based on what he believes rational, self-interested people would agree to under ideal circumstances. To examine Rawls's basic hypothetical question by using his language, consider the following: What would people in an "original position," behind a "veil of ignorance" agree to, with regard to a just society? In other words, in an initial situation in which people had to choose the basic principles of a just society and in which they were truly unbiased – because they did not know the particulars of their social, economic, intellectual, moral, and psychological identities – what principles would they choose? According to Rawls, the principles that unbiased, rational agents would choose are the fundamental principles of justice.

For Rawls, justice means fairness. Two basic principles are implied. The first principle is that each person has an equal right to the most extensive liberty that is consistent with a similar liberty for other people. The second principle is that social and economic inequalities must be arranged so that they are to everyone's advantage and linked to offices and positions that are open to all citizens. This principle means that economic inequality is unfair unless it turns out to be to everyone's advantage. For instance, everyone might be better off if surgeons were paid more than fast food workers. Unlike Marx's theory, for Rawls, justice does not imply absolute economic equality. Justice means fairness.

Let us experiment with Rawls's concept by entertaining three of our own hypothetical examples. Let us assume that we are perfectly unbiased and wish to maximize our rational self-interest. If given a choice between three societies (A, B, and C), which one would we pick? In society A, everyone is guaranteed to make $30,000. In society B, 25% make $30,000, 50% make $60,000 and 25% make $120,000 or more. In society C, 5% make $10,000, 10% make $20,000, 30% make $60,000, 20% make $120,000, 10% make $240,000, and 5% make $480,000 or more. Society A has one class. Society B has three classes and society C has seven. The following chart summarizes these possibilities:

Society A	
%	Salary
100	30K

Society B	
%	Salary
25	120K+
50	60K
25	30K

Society C	
%	Salary
5	480K+
10	240K
20	120K
30	60K
20	30K
10	20K
5	10K

Although these specific numbers and examples are ours, rather than Rawls's, they serve to illustrate Rawls's liberal theory. Rawls's concept of "justice as fairness" implies that rational, unbiased people would pick society B. In this society, even though there is some inequality, "the least advantaged class" is guaranteed a fairly decent standard of living. To accomplish this, however, some redistribution of income is required, to lower the ceiling and raise the floor, so to speak. Thus, in Rawls's modern liberal theory, government policies that decrease huge inequalities – welfare, progressive taxation, and minimum wage laws, for example – are given a theoretical justification based on the idea of fairness.

NOZICK

Robert Nozick (1938-2002) as a conservative libertarian, thinks of justice as market entitlement. Whereas Marx thinks of justice as absolute economic equality and Rawls sees justice as fairness, Nozick believes that individuals are entitled to keep their possessions, as long as they did not obtain them by fraud. Individuals have rights, particularly property rights, which may not rightfully be violated by the state.

Nozick wonders if the state's existence is even justified, in the first place. Although he is not an anarchist – one who believes that all governments are illegitimate – he thinks that only a "minimal state" is morally justified. The state should focus exclusively on protecting citizens from violence, breach of contracts, fraud, theft, etc. A more expansive state is morally unjustified because it will be unnecessarily coercive. A minimal state is right and inspiring.

The minimal night-watchman state must always be aware of its necessary limits. Like an umpire, it must simply enforce the rules rather than interfere in the economic game, so to speak. The free market, with its associated law of supply and demand, should determine what each person or worker gets paid. Radical income redistribution, as in utopian communism or moderate income redistribution, as in modern liberalism, is misguided, according to his libertarian perspective. Taking from the rich to give to the poor, Robin Hood's social project, is unjust according to this point of view. This summarizes Nozick's entitlement view of justice.

Individual Liberty or the Common Good?

Liberals and libertarians emphasize individual liberty as the fundamental human right. Liberals, like Rawls, believe the most basic right is the right to individual liberty. Libertarians, like Nozick, emphasize the individual's right to private property. In recent years, however, some philosophers have wondered if individual liberty is really more important than "the common good." Should the good of humanity, or the nation, or the tribe or the family take precedence over the individual's rights? Philosophers who emphasize "the common good" of the community, as the primary political consideration, are called communitarians. They include such recent influential thinkers as Sandel and Walzer.

Are they right or wrong?

REVIEW QUESTIONS

In order to tackle the tough questions in political philosophy, let us review the key concepts and ideologies.

I CONTRASTING IDEAS

Explain the differences in the following ideas:

1. elitism vs. democracy
2. natural law theory vs. contractarian theory
3. divine right of kings vs. consent of the governed
4. state of nature vs. civil society
5. totalitarianism vs. democracy

II PRELIMINARY QUESTIONS

1. What is the best foundation for government: an ideal form, a natural law, or a social contract?
2. Is civil disobedience or a revolution ever justified? Under what conditions might you approve of these actions?
3. Should we assume that there are basic human rights that existed prior to governments? Why?
4. Explain your list of universal human rights.
5. Is social order more important than individual freedom? Is the opposite view correct? Are they equally important?
6 Is economic equality more important than economic productivity? Is the opposite view correct? Are they equally important?
7. Is it better to have a flat tax or a progressive tax? Why?
8. Should we have more or less censorship in our society? Why?
9. Which philosophers have the best ideas on individual freedom?
10. Which philosophers have the best concepts of social justice?
11. Which philosophers have the most objectionable views? Why?
12. Explain your rank ordering of all 12 of the major political theorists.

III DEEP QUESTIONS

1. What are the essential features of a good society?
2. Is the U.S.A. a good society?
3. What should we preserve or improve in our society?
4. What are the central values in your favorite political party?
5. Where would you locate your view, with regard to the following political spectrum?

The Political Spectrum

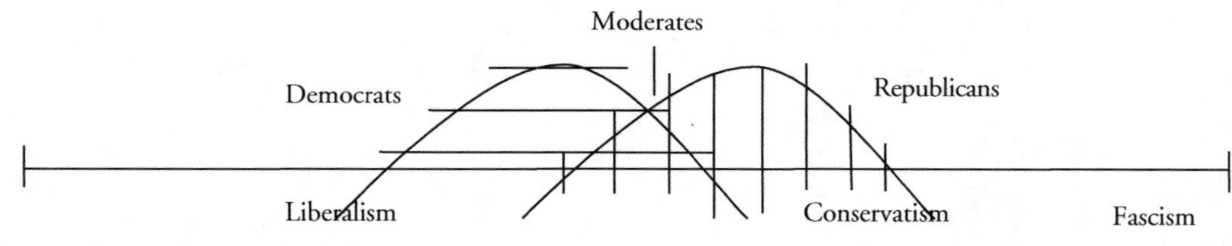

c h a p t e r 4

Metaphysics and Epistemology

In the previous chapters, we noticed the connections between the basic questions in ethics and politics. These questions relate to the nature of the "Good Life" and the essence of a "Good Society." In metaphysics and epistemology, once again, we notice a very close relationship between two domains of philosophy. Metaphysics deals with theories of reality. Epistemology deals with theories of knowledge. The reason for the connection between these areas of philosophy, is that our assumptions about reality impact our beliefs regarding the criteria and procedures for knowledge. Let us examine the basic questions in these philosophical fields.

METAPHYSICAL QUESTIONS

There are a number of key questions in metaphysics. Some of the central questions include the following:

1. What is the nature of ultimate reality?
2. Is there one final reality?
3. Are there two, or many more, ultimately real entities?
4. Is the final reality something physical, mental, or spiritual?
5. Are abstract universal ideas more real than concrete particular things?
6. Do non-physical entities – minds, soul, free-wills, for examples – exist?
7. Is the ultimate reality something permanent or something that is constantly changing?
8. How are "mind" and "matter" related?
9. What is the difference between "reality" and "appearance"?

EPISTEMOLOGICAL QUESTIONS

Some of the key questions in epistemology include the following:

1. What is the difference between "knowledge" and "opinion"?
2. What are the criteria for knowledge?
3. Do we know anything with absolute certainty?
4. What are the most reliable sources for real knowledge?
5. Are all claims to knowledge distorted by personal or cultural bias?
6. Does purely objective knowledge exist?
7. How do we know that we know?

These questions about reality and knowledge are among the most fundamental sorts of questions that are tackled by philosophers. The nature of reality and the ways in which it can be known, form the basis for our most fundamental assumptions in science, religion, art, ethics, and politics. In science, for example, we assume that all events are determined by prior material causes. In ethics, on the other hand, we tend to assume that certain human actions are based on a "free will" rather than a set of material causes. Are both of these assumptions compatible? This raises a metaphysical question regarding the status of non-physical entities. In many of the world's religions, there is a belief in one or more deities. Can we know that there is a God? This, to be sure, raises an epistemological question regarding the criteria for knowledge, as well as a metaphysical question concerning the ultimate nature of reality. In politics we discover conservative and liberal perspectives in the mass media, frequently in the form of very heated discussions. Is there any pure objective truth in politics? Are all media organizations infected by different forms of political bias? This, of course, is a variation of a major epistemological question regarding the nature of objectivity. Furthermore, in the art world of the twentieth century, we encounter quite a few "abstract" images in contrast to the almost exclusively representational images of the past. Are abstract forms more real than concrete physical things? This, to be sure, is a metaphysical question. Thus, in short, our scientific, ethical, religious, political, and aesthetic beliefs are connected with our assumptions about the nature of reality and knowledge. This implies that metaphysics and epistemology are foundational areas in our study of philosophy.

TYPES OF METAPHYSICAL THEORIES

Although there are several theories of reality in the area of metaphysics, the following types of theories are the major ones: materialism, idealism, dualism, and neutralism. They may be summarized in the following way:

1. MATERIALISM – the view that the ultimate reality is matter
2. IDEALISM – the view that the ultimate reality is mind, or spirit, or form
3. DUALISM – the view that two ultimately real (but different) substances exist, namely, mind and matter
4. NEUTRALISM – the view that mind and matter are not different entities but different descriptions of the same substance

These theories also come in different forms depending on how many ultimately real substances are assumed to exist. Monism is the view that only one reality exists. Dualism is the view that two basic realities exist and pluralism is the idea that many ultimately real entities exist. The theory of idealism, for instance, may be set forth in a monistic or a pluralistic form.

TYPES OF EPISTEMOLOGICAL THEORIES

Theories in epistemology revolve around the ways in which true beliefs may be justified so as to count as "knowledge." They may be summarized in the following way:

1. DOGMATISM – the view that authority (unquestioned belief) is the source of knowledge
2. RATIONALISM – the view that reason is the basis for knowledge
3. EMPIRICISM – the view that experience (sensory perception) is the basis for knowledge
4. PRAGMATISM – the view that successful action is the basis for knowledge
5. SKEPTICISM – the view that there is no knowledge since truth claims are never fully justified

A few epistemologists believe that there is only one ultimate source of knowledge. For the most part, however, the basic arguments have to do with the best priority system to justify the truth of our beliefs. Which source is the primary one in justifying our claims to knowledge? According to dogmatism, knowledge comes from authority. Traditional experts, academic scholars, religious leaders, parents, and teachers are critical because dogmas (unquestioned beliefs) are essential. According to rationalism, real knowledge comes from rational ideas. Concepts are most essential. Rationalists frequently use formal logic or mathematics as models of pure reason leading to knowledge. According to empiricism, real knowledge comes from experience or sensory perceptions. Empiricists focus on careful observations and gather sensory data as the basis for justifying claims to knowledge. According to pragmatism, real knowledge comes from actions. Successful practices are most vital in acquiring knowledge. We must make continual adjustments in our set of beliefs in order to keep pace with a changing world. According to skepticism, all so-called "real knowledge" is opinion. Continuous skeptical doubts are most crucial in unmasking all claims to pure, objective, certain universal knowledge.

What is the ultimate nature of reality? What is the best way to gather real knowledge? These questions lead us into the fundamental areas of philosophical inquiry. They invite us to consider the theories and arguments of the great philosophers throughout history.

PRE-SOCRATICS

Philosophers who came before Socrates (470-399 B.C.), the famous teacher of Plato, are referred to as the pre-Socratic philosophers. They spent a good deal of time wondering about the ultimate nature of reality and the best ways of knowing it. Instead of simply accepting the mythology of the Greek poet, Homer, as the authoritative source for explaining the universe, the philosophers tried to use reason. Thales, who is generally regarded as the first philosopher in the western tradition, raised the key question which philosophers and scientists have wrestled with over the years. The central question is the following: What is the basic "stuff" that underlies everything we experience in the world?

This question is sometimes referred to as the problem of "the one and the many." We encounter many things on a daily basis – plants, rocks, cats, trees, sand, stars, people, etc. What unifies these many things? Is everything a manifestation of one fundamental substance? What could this substance be?

Thales (624-545 B.C.), along with several Pre-Socratics tried to answer this question. For Thales, the basic substance was water. Even though this turned out to be a wrong answer, it was not a bad hypothesis. After all, water can appear in many states. Perhaps this substance is flexible enough to appear in all the forms which characterize reality, Thales might have reasoned. At any rate, it frequently happens in philosophy and science that questions are just as important as answers. The questions that Thales raised regarding the possibility of explaining the complex world of our sensory experiences with a basic underlying substance, is the question that signals the beginning of metaphysics. Modern metaphysics and physics are still exploring this question.

Thales's water theory encountered competition. One of his students, Anaximander (610-547 B.C.), claimed that the basic stuff must be even more elementary than water. Anaximenes (545 B.C.) set forth the idea that air was the basic substance. When it is condensed it becomes wind, then clouds, water, earth, and stone. On the other hand, rarefied air becomes fire. When we consider that air allows life to exist, we realize that this theory, although wrong, was reasonable, and not simply "hot air."

Pythagoras (580-500 B.C.) set forth the view that all things exist in accordance with number. The universe is a manifestation of order and harmony. Its ultimate reality can only be known through reason, which puts us in touch with that which is eternal and unchanging. Pythagoras founded a school of thought that made a religion out of mathematics and contributed to the theory of music.

Heraclitus (535-475 B.C) was another interesting pre-Socratic thinker with an important theory of reality. For him, everything is a manifestation of fire. Everything is constantly changing. Permanence is an illusion. Since the nature of fire is to cause change, it is the fundamental substance in the universe. In our world, one cannot "step in the same river twice," according to Heraclitus. This was his way of dramatizing the centrality of change. Change, for him, however, was not random. It was determined by the logos – the principle of order in the universe. Thus, the universe exhibits orderly change. The logos is in the flux.

Parmenides (515-450 B.C.) opposed this theory. For him, the ultimate reality is Eternal, Unchanging, Being. Being is an indivisible and undifferentiated whole. The world of sensory experiences seems to reveal the existence of motion or change. This world, however, is merely a world of appearances. The truly real world is the world that is disclosed through our reason. This real world is permanent and unchanging.

At this juncture, we seem to be at an impasse. Is reality (or being) constantly changing, as Heraclitus maintained? Is it better to think of reality as permanently unchanging, as Parmenides insisted? Is change the very essence of reality or simply an illusion brought about by the limitations of our senses? The next major pre-Socratic philosopher provided us with a mediating theory. According to Empedocles, true reality is both changing and unchanging because of its basic structure. That is to say, reality is composed of four fundamental elements: air, earth, fire, and water. These basic elements are unchanging but the ways in which they combine are constantly changing. Permanence and change are thus, equally real. Although we have come a long way in our knowledge of the natural sciences, the modern organic chemist still uses four basic elements – carbon, hydrogen, nitrogen, and oxygen – in explaining life processes. Empedocles' idea was an important contribution to our understanding of things.

Another important pre-Socratic philosopher was Anaxagoras (500-428 B.C.). He put forth the distinction between mind and matter. The material universe is made up of four basic kinds of particles, but the source of all motion is MIND. MIND is separate from matter because it does not contain any mixture of elements. It is present in all things. It animates everything. It did not create the material world, but it is responsible for shaping it. Anaxagoras' concept of MIND is similar to the Judeo-Christian idea of God, if we subtract the idea of "personality" from the concept of the ultimate reality.

A very different view of the ultimate reality is present in the theory of Democritus (460-370 B.C.). This pre-Socratic philosopher believed that everything is composed of physical atoms. Atoms are very tiny, indivisible, eternal, and uncreated entities that are forever in motion. All of our experiences are based on the ways in which atoms combine with other atoms. Growth and decay, for examples, are to be explained by the bonding and disassembling of atoms. Atomic connections and disconnections, however, are determined by physical laws. Thus, the universe is predictable because all events are determined by the sizes, shapes, directions, and speeds of the atoms as they form a variety of combinations.

PLATO

Plato set forth comprehensive theories of reality and knowledge. With regard to his theory of reality, he favored idealism. With respect to his theory of knowledge, he supported rationalism. His metaphysics and epistemology, like his ethics and politics, are logically tied together.

To begin with, let us examine his theory of reality. For Plato, the real world is the world of permanent, abstract, conceptual, eternal, universal, ideal forms. The world of appearances, on the other hand, is the world of changing, concrete, perceptual, temporal, particular actual things. The abstract world of pure, universal, ideal forms is vastly superior to the concrete world of imperfect, particular, actual things.

Let us explore some physical illustrations of Plato's metaphysical conception. The concept of "circularity," for instance, is an abstract universal ideal form or pattern. Mathematicians would define it as a set of points equidistant from a central point. There are several circular things that we experience with our physical senses quite frequently. Examples of circularity would include things like balls, coins, rings, pizzas, doughnuts, etc. The abstract concept of circularity, as understood by the mind, is unchanging. On the other hand, the concrete illustrations of circularity – balls, coins, rings, pizzas, doughnuts, etc. – are constantly changing. Balls lose air. Coins and rings get chipped and change color. Pizzas and doughnuts lose their circularity as soon as we get our hands on them. Can "circularity" itself ever change? The answer is obviously no. This means that our mental conceptions inhabit a realm of being that is much more stable than our physical perceptions. The world of abstract universal concepts is the world that we can truly get to know with our minds. The world of concrete particular things, on the other hand, is, unfortunately, a world of changing perceptions based on the data from our senses. It can never lead us to the light of knowledge.

Plato illustrated this idea by giving us the most famous allegory in the history of philosophy – the allegory of the cave. According to this philosophical parable, the masses, who are governed by their physical senses, are like prisoners in a deep dark cave. These prisoners are restricted to seeing the shadows of objects as they are reflected on the wall of the cave. A liberated prisoner, moving higher in the cave, might glimpse the real objects, whose shadows are reflected on the wall of the cave. A fully liberated prisoner, after escaping from the cave, would have a much better understanding of the objects which were vaguely seen in the cave. After getting accustomed to life outside the cave, the fully liberated former prisoner would be in a position to appreciate the sun's light, by means of which the objects of the real world become visible.

The allegory of the cave illustrated Plato's concepts of reality and knowledge. The real world – the world outside the cave – is the world of unchanging abstract universal concepts and forms. This world can be known by the mind. The cave, on the other hand, is the world of changing concrete particular things and their representations. This is the world of appearances which is "known" by the physical senses. To summarize Plato's concepts, let us examine the following diagram:

LEVELS OF REALITY	POSSIBLE EXAMPLES		DEGREES OF KNOWING
	GOODNESS		
1. FORMS	TRUTH	BEAUTY	KNOWING
2. CONCEPTS	F=MA	SYMMETRY	THINKING
	LIGHT		
3. THINGS	car	Miss America	BELIEVING
4. SHADOWS	picture of a car	Miss America on television	IMAGINING

In this diagram, the first two levels represent the intelligible world. The third and fourth levels represent the visible world. For Plato, the intelligible world is the real world. The visible world is "the cave," the world of appearances. Forms and concepts represent reality. Things and shadows are at a much lower level. The ultimate forms are Goodness, Truth, and Beauty. In the realm of ideas, for instance, a formula like force equals mass times acceleration, Newton's second law of motion, is a conceptual representation of truth. A physical thing, like a car, is a physical representation of scientific truths. A picture of a car is a physical representation of a physical object.

A similar set of levels can be discerned with respect to beauty. Beauty, like Truth and Goodness, is a pure, ideal universal form or pattern. A concept like symmetry is a conceptual representation of beauty. A particular person, like Miss America, is a physical representation of beauty. An appearance of Miss America on television is a physical representation of a particular person. In all cases, concrete particulars are not as real as abstract universals. The picture of a car, and the car itself, will deteriorate with time. Miss America will undergo a similar fate. Seventy years from now, as she enters her nursing home, we can imagine the ways in which her physical features will change. A rusty car and a wrinkled Miss America, however, do not change the concepts of truth and beauty, respectively. Truth and Beauty are permanent universal ideal forms. All true statements, propositions, and formulas participate in Truth itself. All beautiful people, poems, and plays participate in Beauty itself.

For Plato, Goodness, Truth, and Beauty are the ultimate objects of knowledge. They are known through our rational intuition and serve as the necessary bases for our moral, scientific, and aesthetic thinking. Particular physical objects, which change and decay, are, at best, pale representations of these ultimate realities. Physical objects, strictly speaking, cannot be known since knowledge, according to Plato, is reserved for stable, timeless realities – the forms. Physical entities may be objects of imagination or belief. Knowledge, however, comes from the mind, not the physical senses.

Plato's theories of reality and knowledge had a huge impact on our culture. Some philosophers think that philosophy is nothing but a series of footnotes to Plato. Idealists in metaphysics and rationalists in epistemology see him as a founding father. In religion, the idea of the immortal soul, in contrast to the perishable physical body, is a Platonic way of seeing reality. In art, the quest for pure ideal forms and the use of abstract patterns reminds us of Plato's perspective. Even our ordinary language pays tribute to Plato. We refer to a "Platonic relationship," for instance, as one that involves an exclusively mental (rather than physical) relationship. Thus, Plato's views on reality and knowledge have affected us greatly.

ARISTOTLE

Aristotle, Plato's most famous student, put forward some contrasting ideas in the areas of metaphysics and epistemology. His metaphysical theory is focused on naturalism, while his epistemological theory is based on empiricism. Like Plato, Aristotle greatly impacted the history of ideas.

According to Aristotle's naturalism, the real world is the world of nature. Abstract universal forms are only real if they are embedded in concrete particular things. The basic principle of Aristotle's metaphysics is that each thing is a combination of matter and form. Everything is made out of some sort of stuff (matter). Nothing comes from nothing. Everything has some type of pattern (form). Without form a thing would not be the particular kind of thing that it is. The form is the thing's essential nature. Things also undergo change and, for Aristotle, each change is directed toward some end or goal.

To understand things, and the ways in which they change, we must take into account the four types of causes: formal, material, efficient, and final. The formal cause is the thing's essence. The material cause is the stuff from which the thing is made. The efficient cause is what produced the thing. (This is our standard meaning of the idea of a "cause.") The final cause is the ultimate end or purpose that the thing serves.

Let us consider a statue and a baseball as examples of things to analyze using Aristotle's four types of causes. If the form is a statue, the material cause might be marble, the efficient cause would be the sculptor's chisel and the final cause would be the production of an art object. If the form is a baseball, the material cause might be leather and cork, the efficient cause might be a factory and the final cause would be the production of an object for recreation.

But what about natural objects? A typical example is the acorn. The acorn is a potential tree. An actual oak tree started out as an acorn. This example illustrates that in nature, there is clearly a movement from potentiality to actuality. Actuality, in a sense is the ultimate cause, or end, or purpose of change. Pure actuality is the unmoved mover. This, for Aristotle, is the reality of god. This god, or unmoved mover, however, is not the same as the personal God in the monotheistic religions, like Judaism, Islam, or Christianity. Aristotle's god is the unmoved mover, or the unchanged changer, which is the goal of all reality.

Reality may be seen as a continuum from possibility to pure actuality. Matter is pure possibility and god is pure actuality. Nature exists between these polarities. Natural entities strive to realize their potentialities. Changing imperfect beings seek to become like god by fulfilling their possibilities. In the physical realm, minerals, vegetables, and animals exist. Everything that exists may be understood in terms of a set of basic categories: essence, quantity, quality, relationship, place, time, constitution, posture, activity, and passivity.

What about human beings? For Aristotle, humans are rational animals. The human soul is the form of the body. It keeps the body in order and provides it with a goal or purpose to pursue. To be more precise, Aristotle thinks in terms of three types of human souls – vegetative, animal, and rational. The vegetative soul deals with nourishment and reproduction. The animal soul deals with sensing and moving. The rational soul is a pure, immortal spiritual soul that allows humans to engage in speculative thinking – about reality as a whole – and in this respect approach the divine nature.

How do human beings get knowledge? As an empiricist, Aristotle believes that, for the most part, humans get knowledge through sensory perceptions. Our senses give us the experiences or data that we use to compare and contrast with other experiences. Things that are similar belong in the same general category – genus. Specific differences give rise to species. Using reasoning, based on cause and effect relationships, along with noticing the contrasts between possibility and actuality, etc., we learn about the imperfect, changing, real natural world. Intuition, however, is needed to account for our knowledge of the most basic logical principle – the principle of non-contradiction – and the most basic ultimate reality, pure actuality or God.

PLOTINUS

Plotinus (205-270 B.C.) set forth a mystical view of reality, which was inspired by Plato's philosophy. According to this mystical Neoplatonism, reality may be viewed as a series of concentric circles in the following order: The One, spirit, soul, and the material world. Reality emanates from The One. The One, according to Plotinus, is indescribable and indefinable. Any attempted definition of The One would place limitations on this infinite, ultimate reality and thus distort its true essence. Titles for The One include the following: God, the First Existent, the Infinite, and the Absolute. The One is like the sun, which illuminates all things.

The One creates everything. It does not do this by a conscious choice, since it is not personal. It would be better to say that everything proceeds from The One by necessity. Spirit, or Divine Mind, or Intellect, is the first emanation from The One. Soul emanates from Spirit. It is the realm that mediates between the spiritual realm and the material realm. Individual persons have souls, which are aspects of the World Soul. The human soul is immortal and will be reincarnated. The final emanation is the material world, with its multiplicity, which contrasts sharply with the perfect unity of the divine.

The material world is the lowest type of reality in the hierarchy of being. From the perspective of Plotinus, it is not really real since it is so far removed from the central transcendent core of reality – The One. Comparing the material world to The One, is like comparing darkness to light or evil to goodness.

The material world is the lowest object of knowledge. The highest source of knowledge is The One, which can only be known by mystical intuition. A direct mystical experience, in which the soul touches God, is the greatest moment in life. Philosophical contemplation, which helps us to understand the eternal intelligible world of forms, is also a great experience for the human soul. Observing aspects of the material world with our senses, however, is the lowest form of knowledge since it deals with temporal, changing, particular things. Like Plato, Plotinus thinks of the material world as an inferior realm.

ST. AUGUSTINE

St. Augustine adopted Plato's theory of reality and put a Christian spin on it. His concept of reality may be illustrated in the following manner:

Ideal World:	**God**	**soul**	**universals**
Natural World:	**matter**	**body**	**particulars**

Augustine was deeply impacted by the Neo-platonic mysticism of Plotinus, according to which the ultimate realm of being was an immaterial reality. Plato and Plotinus provided Augustine with an idealistic framework of ideas that blended philosophical rationality with Christianity. For him, true philosophy is compatible with theology because reason and revelation are complimentary.

God is the most excellent and sublime reality. He is eternal and unchanging. Wisdom, knowledge, power, and goodness are some of His essential attributes, which are perfectly united in His being. In fact, for Augustine, God is Being itself. Things that exist in the material world derive their reality from God, insofar as they are finite reflections of God's infinite eternal thoughts. God, for Augustine, is the supreme object of love and the final standard for Truth.

The material world is God's creation. God created it out of nothing. This doctrine of creation departs from the ideas of Plato and Plotinus, however, in some respects. Plato believed that God (the Demiurge) as a great artist, created the patterns in nature by imitating the ideal forms and rearranging materials which existed independently and eternally. Plotinus saw the material world as a necessary emanation from God or The One. God is so packed with reality that this reality had to overflow necessarily. The material world, for Plotinus, is thus an extension of God. In contrast to these ideas, Augustine held that the material world is the result of God's free creative action. There is therefore a clear distinction between God, as creator, and the material world, as the creation. Matter did not always exist. Ideal forms do not exist independently of God's mind, according to Augustine. God's creative intelligence is the source of everything. God implanted seminal principles into the natural world and thereby allowed for the potentiality of all species to reproduce themselves. The mind of God is the ultimate cause for all things and animals in the natural world.

Augustine's concept of creation, to some degree, departs from the Platonic view. His concepts of incarnation and resurrection also depart from Platonic idealism. The Christian idea of incarnation means that Jesus is God "in the flesh." The resurrection of Jesus means that Jesus Christ's body, in some form, was reunited with his soul after death. Taken together, the doctrines of creation, incarnation, and resurrection seem to indicate that the material world is not a "metaphysical slum," so to speak, but an object of intense love and concern for God. The Creator identifies Himself intensely with His creation. From a purely Platonic viewpoint, the world of pure ideal forms and the world of imperfect physical things are so different, that it would be extremely hard to imagine a god wishing to be "materialized" by taking on a human body, at birth, and keeping some form of it, eternally, in heaven. As a Christian, however, Augustine affirmed these doctrines and, consequently, modified his Platonic idealism.

Platonic rationalism, with regard to the theory of knowledge, profoundly impacted Augustine. Reason for both is the basis for knowing. In contrast to skepticism, which holds that there are no propositions that are absolutely certain, Augustine believed that reason indicated otherwise. Reason is certain about the principle of non-contradiction, for instance, according to which a thing cannot be the same as its opposite. Examples include the following: Hot is not cold, tall is not short, etc. Reason knows, moreover, that this principle of non-contradiction is eternally true. Reason also shows that another certainty exists – the certainty of our existence, which is confirmed in every act of doubting. Thus, reason refutes skepticism.

Reasoning is also superior to sensing in the process of knowing. Augustine believed that sensing is the lowest form of knowing. It gives us the lowest degree of certainty. Things that we sense are constantly changing and our perceptions change. Sense perceptions change from sense to sense and from person to person. An apple, for instance, can look great but taste terrible. One person may perceive it as sweet and another may perceive it as sour. Two apples plus seven apples, however, always equal nine apples. Two plus seven equals nine. Our sensory data about the apples change. Our mental apprehension of the mathematical relationships, however, gives rise to eternal truths. Eternal and necessary truths come from the mind or the soul. The light of eternal reason, which stems from divine illumination, informs us of these sorts of truth.

ST. THOMAS AQUINAS

St. Thomas Aquinas put a Christian spin on the philosophy of Aristotle. In this way, he blended religious faith and philosophical reason. His view of reality may be represented in the following way:

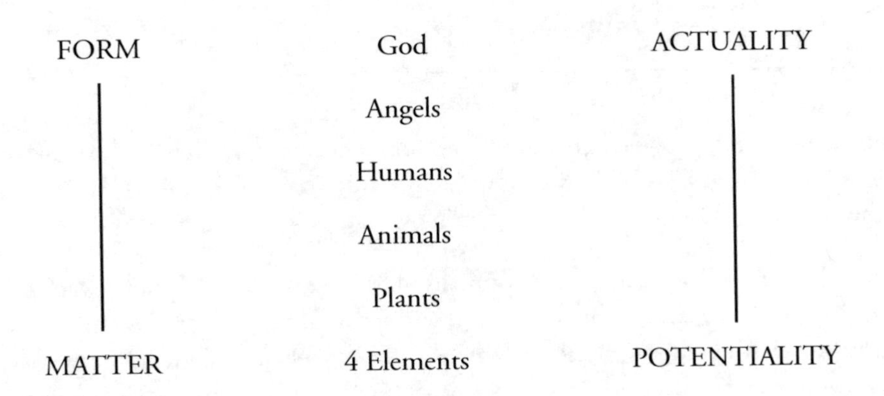

God is the highest point in the great chain of being. God's absolute perfection is reflected in the full range of the created order. Each created being reveals a partial aspect of the limitless perfections of God. All potentiality is fulfilled in the perfect actuality of God.

Angels are next in line in the hierarchy of beings. According to Aquinas, angels are immaterial intelligences. They fill in the gap between God and humans. Human beings are lower than angels. Whereas angels are particular intelligences or spirits, humans are made up of both material and spiritual components. Below humans are animals, then plants, and finally the four elements, namely, earth, air, fire, and water.

Human beings are roughly in the middle of the great chain of being. A human being is a unity of soul and body. Without the soul, the body would have no form or structure. Without the body, the soul would have no way of sensing the world. The soul accounts for the human faculties of intellect and will, while the body provides the sense organs for knowledge. Unlike the Platonic view, Aquinas saw a connection between the world of forms and the world of matter. This relatively high regard for matter is more conducive to the idea that matter could be a suitable residence for the divine than the Platonic outlook. Thus, Aquinas believed that Aristotle's naturalistic view was a better partner for religious faith than Plato's idealistic view.

St. Thomas Aquinas also followed Aristotle's lead in dealing with the nature of human knowledge. Both thinkers were empiricists. They believed that knowledge is based on sensory perception. That is to say, there is nothing in the mind that was not, at first, in the senses. The senses deal with particular things. The mind gives us universal concepts. These universals, however, are abstracted from the particulars. Without sensing circular things, for instance, we would not understand the universal concept of circularity. Without seeing beautiful things and people, we would not understand the concept of beauty. Thus, with regard to the way in which we get knowledge, the concrete particulars of our sensory experience are vital.

DESCARTES

René Descartes (1596-1650), the father of modern philosophy, focused on developing a theory of knowledge which provided the foundation for his theory of reality. With regard to his theory of knowledge, his key problem was to investigate the basis for certainty. His central question was the following: Do we ever know anything with absolute certainty?

The scientific revolution shook the foundations of our so-called "knowledge" of the world. Copernicus, in 1543, articulated the view that the sun, rather than the earth, was the center of our universe. Kepler, in 1609, showed that the planets move in elliptical (rather than circular) orbits. Moreover, Galileo used his telescope, in 1610, to discover that there were more than seven heavenly bodies. Taken together, these new scientific beliefs challenged the traditional dogmas of the time about the nature of the universe.

Descartes also had personal reasons for his quest for certainty. After finishing his studies, he felt restless and had a strong desire to see the world. He joined the army to accomplish this. After studying "the great book of the world," he realized that different cultures have very different customs. A lot of what we take to be knowledge is based on our customs. How do we know that our customs are really valid? Maybe other cultures are right. In reflecting on his previous academic experience, Descartes remembered that he studied philosophy at college. Philosophy, however, is filled with many different perspectives. How do we know which perspective is right? Moreover, as he aged, Descartes noticed that his tastes changed. A lot of our beliefs are based on our tastes. How do we know what sort of tastes we will have in the future? With different social customs, philosophical perspectives, and personal tastes, is there any hope of finding any objective universal truth that we can know with certainty?

Mathematics, he thought, might deliver us from uncertainty and lead us to pure objectivity. After all, in geometry, for example, the conclusion follows necessarily from the basic axioms that we use in the process of reasoning. A similar method, Descartes hoped, should provide us with a solid procedure for reasoning. Descartes, the founder of analytic geometry, set forth four principal rules of a method for finding truth. First, accept only clear and distinct ideas. Second, break down problems into manageable components. Third, be orderly and begin with the simple parts before moving on to the more complex components. Finally, review all the steps in the process in a thorough manner. If we observe these rules for reasoning, we will be on the road to finding truth.

But where do we begin? Is there any proposition that we clearly know to be true which could serve as a rock-solid foundation for other truths? In order to discover this, Descartes adopted a procedure called "methodic doubt." This procedure required him to doubt everything that was logically possible to doubt. If any proposition proved to be beyond all possible doubt, then that proposition would have to be regarded as "certain."

Is there any proposition immune from doubt? Descartes used two conjectures, the dream conjecture and the evil demon conjecture, to test this idea. According to the dream conjecture, many propositions that we believe could be doubted simply because we could be dreaming. Furthermore, according to the evil demon conjecture, many statements that we believe to be true, could turn out to be false because an evil demon might be deceiving us in a systematic way. Taken together, these bizarre conjectures imply that just about any proposition could be doubted.

Now we should clarify the nature of Descartes' methodic doubt. First of all, it is meant to be taken as a theoretical and logical strategy to see if there are any propositions that are absolutely certain. Descartes' methodic doubt should not, therefore, be seen as a practical and psychological procedure. On a purely practical level, Descartes realized that we are forced to act as if we are certain about several things and that doubting them could cause trouble. Suppose we entertained doubts about stopping at the next red light while driving? This kind of doubt, of course, would be extremely silly. Continuously doubting everything is not meant to be practical advice. Descartes realized that his conjectures were bizarre. The point of them, however, is to show that just about every proposition, on a theoretical level at least, could be doubted.

Is any proposition beyond any possible doubt? At this point, Descartes offered an example which became one of the most famous "one-liners" in the history of philosophy: "I think, therefore I am." Suppose we tried to doubt our own existence. Doubting implies thought and thought implies existence. Thus, it is logically impossible to doubt that we exist. The more we doubt our existence, the more we prove it. At last Descartes found what he was looking for, namely, an absolutely certain proposition that could serve as a foundational belief for his other beliefs to rest upon.

Are there any other absolutely certain basic beliefs? Descartes held that "God" and "the mind" as his essential self, are absolutely certain. He tried to prove God's existence by relying on several arguments. One of them runs as follows: God is the infinite perfect being. To exist in reality is more perfect than to exist merely in the mind. Therefore, by necessary implication, God must exist. Descartes also used his method of logical deduction to try to prove another foundational belief – that his mind is his essential self. Once again he used his methodic doubt. If we really tried to doubt the body's existence, Descartes claimed, we could imagine, without contradicting ourselves, that our bodies did not exist. On the other hand, no matter how hard we tried to doubt the mind's existence, we could never doubt it. Doubting implies thinking and thinking requires a mind. This indicated to Descartes that, unlike his body, his mind was his essential self.

Descartes believed that this epistemological journey in search of absolute certainty yielded metaphysical truth. For Descartes, methodic doubt revealed that there are two types of entities: mind and matter. The key feature of matter is that it occupies space. In a word, it has "extension." The key feature of mind is "thought." Whereas material substances, including the body, are subjected to the laws of physics; mental substances are immaterial things and are, therefore, not subjected to the physical laws.

Descartes' rationalism ended up by establishing the metaphysical theory called dualism. According to dualism, mind and matter are two different entities. Religion deals with the realm of mind or spirit. In this realm, ideas like the freedom of the will and the immortality of the soul, have their place. Science, on the other hand, deals with the realm of matter. In this realm, the universal natural laws govern all physical phenomena. Thus, in Descartes' view, religion and science need not be in conflict since they deal with separate realities.

HOBBES

Thomas Hobbes attacked Descartes' metaphysical theory of dualism by putting forward his own theory of reality called, materialism. His chief task was to use Galileo's physics as a model to explain every aspect of reality. Hobbes coupled materialism (his theory of reality) with empiricism (his theory of knowledge).

Hobbes's materialism hinged on the idea that reality is nothing but matter in motion. All of reality can be divided into kinds of bodies – natural and political. Natural bodies include things like living organisms, rocks, and planets. These are studied in the physical sciences. Political bodies are artificial bodies. These are studied in political science. The philosopher's job is to examine the principles of these sciences in the most general way. In examining the human body, for instance, the philosopher should think of it, like any other entity in the universe, as a complex machine.

In accounting for human knowledge, Hobbes reduced all thinking to perception. Perception itself, like everything in the universe, is ultimately about matter in motion. Motion without, produces motion within. That is to say, various sorts of motion in the external world cause motions within the brain. These motions in the brain – "phantasms," to use Hobbes' word – start off as sensations from our sensory organs. They account for our understanding of all the qualities in the world – colors, tastes, textures, tones, odors, etc. When the internal motions in the brain linger, even after the external object which caused them is no longer there, we refer to this as imagination or memory. Memory and imagination, for Hobbes, are nothing more than "decaying sense." Even complex thinking is nothing more than a sequence of perceptions. Unlike other animals, humans use words to refer to perceptions. Reasoning is nothing more than adding and subtracting the consequences of general names for our particular perceptions. Abstract universal concepts, like Truth or Beauty, do not exist in some Platonic realm of pure ideal forms or in the mind of St. Augustine's God. All ideas, for Hobbes, must be traced back to their source in sensory perception.

Hobbes' materialistic account of thinking also applies to all human actions. He believed that all events are determined by physical laws. Therefore, involuntary as well as voluntary actions are determined by prior physical causes. He distinguished between vital and voluntary motions. Vital motions are linked to automatic involuntary actions, such as breathing and digesting. Voluntary motions are connected to voluntary actions like speaking to friends or picking a style of clothing. For Hobbes, even voluntary actions are determined by physical causes. He claimed that voluntary motions start off as "endeavors." Endeavors are caused by perceptions and include desires and aversions. A desire is an endeavor toward an object. An aversion is an endeavor away from the object. Love means desire and hate refers to aversion. Good refers to desire and evil refers to aversion. A deliberation is nothing more than an alternation of desires and aversions. Willing is nothing more than the last aversion or desire that is left after a deliberation. In this way, Hobbes' materialism replaced the idea of a "free will" with a set of physical causes.

Hobbes' materialism also took "God" out of the metaphysical realm. Whereas he believed that nature's ultimate cause could be a God, he insisted that we could never have any meaningful idea of a nonphysical substance. The very idea of a "spirit," for instance, would have to be pictured as a very thin and transparent physical substance in order to make any sense. Thus, a full-scale metaphysical materialism explains everything strictly in terms of physical substances in motion.

SPINOZA

Benedict (Baruch) Spinoza (1632-1677) set forth a very different theory of reality from Descartes and Hobbes. His theory may be thought of as a kind of neutralism – or neutral monism. According to Spinoza's neutralism, the ultimate reality may be seen as Substance, or Nature, or God.

Substance, for Spinoza, is self-sufficient and logically independent of any other entity. Substance, or God, is absolutely infinite and has infinite attributes. Substance exists eternally and necessarily. Without Substance, or God, nothing can exist or be conceived. Mind and matter are two ways in which Substance manifests itself to human beings. Mind and matter are not two different things, but two ways of describing one and the same thing – Substance. The structures and connections of ideas is the same as the structures and connections between things. Logical connections are like causal connections. Nothing can be understood in isolation. Ideas and events must be understood in terms of their conceptual or factual relationships. Everything, of course, is related to the totality of reality, or Nature, or God.

Spinoza's neutral monism was an attempt to solve the mind-body problem in metaphysics. Descartes' dualism left us with a vexing problem regarding the way in which the mind affects the body and the body affects the mind. Descartes tried to solve the problem of interaction by using "the pineal gland," located at the base of the brain, as the intermediary entity to explain the mind-body interaction. But this did not really solve the problem of how spiritual and physical substances interact. Hobbes tried to solve the problem by getting rid of the spiritual or mental realm altogether. According to Hobbes' materialism, mental events are really physical events and these, ultimately, refer to nothing but matter in motion. But this seems to deny an essential part of reality. With Spinoza's theory, however, the problem seems to go away. If mind and matter are simply two different ways of talking about the same thing, there is no problem with trying to explain how they connect. It would be like asking how "the commander in chief" is related to "the head of state." Since both terms refer to one and the same person, the president, the problem goes away. In like manner, Spinoza's neutral monism seems to dissolve the mind-body problem without denying the reality of each component of reality. Mind and matter, on this view, are not different substances by different modes of Substance.

Spinoza's neutral monism has interesting scientific, religious, and ethical implications. With respect to science, it sets up the idea that there is nothing contingent in nature. Nature follows necessary universal laws that flow from Substance or God. With respect to religion, it holds the view that God is the complete system of reality which is changeless and infinite. With respect to ethics, it puts forth the idea that the "Good Life" is one that contains continuous, supreme, and everlasting happiness as a natural consequence of the intellectual love of God. Furthermore, since "God" is the logically necessary system of the whole of Nature, religious devotion and scientific investigation are different sides of the same coin, so to speak. Einstein, who believed that God does not play dice with the universe, found Spinoza's neutral monism, which is a version of pantheism, to be quite inspirational.

Spinoza's theory of knowledge is a form of rationalism. At the lowest level of knowledge is opinion or imagination, which comes from sensory experience. The second level is based on reason. Reason means understanding the universal chain of causes for things and logical deductions from axioms which are self-evident. Spinoza thought that geometry was the model for all truth and used this method of logical deduction as the way to communicate philosophical truth in the form of logically-necessary propositions. The highest level of knowledge is rational intuition. It is an integrated vision of the whole of reality. From this perspective, all true statements exhibit logical coherence and all things are understood from the standpoint of eternity.

LEIBNIZ

Gottfried Wilhelm Leibniz (1646-1716) followed Descartes and Spinoza in developing a theory of knowledge based on reason. Like the rationalists before him, he believed that the ideas in logic and mathematics came from reason. Sense experience never allows us to understand certainty and necessity. Since some of our knowledge deals with truths that are certain and necessary, this indicates that these ideas are built into the mind itself. In other words, some ideas are innate. The mind discovers them within itself.

The mind discovers truths that are certain, necessary, and universal. Innate ideas, like the principle of identity and the principle of non-contradiction, are latent in the mind. Sense experience, however, allows latent knowledge to become explicit knowledge. For example, the mind knows that a thing is equal to itself (the principle of identity) and that a thing is not equal to its opposite (the principle of non-contradiction). Sense experience shows that four tall boys are not equal to four short girls. Experience allows us to make the form of knowledge that is latent in the mind, concrete and explicit.

Leibniz also carved out a very important distinction in the theory of knowledge between truths of reason and truths of fact. Later philosophers would call truths of reason ANALYTIC propositions and truths of fact SYNTHETIC propositions. Analytic propositions are true by definition. Synthetic propositions are true, if they are verified by the facts in the world. Examples of analytic propositions include the following: Bachelors are unmarried males. Widows have dead husbands. Examples of synthetic propositions include the following: Bachelors are relatively messy. Palm Beach widows are rich. The truth of analytic propositions is based on the meanings of the terms, independently of observation. No observation, after all, could ever prove that a bachelor was not a male. On the other hand, the truth of synthetic propositions is based on the factual data in the world that we observe. To determine that a group of bachelors tends to be messy or that many widows, in a certain location, tend to be rich, we would have to do extensive surveys to confirm these truth claims. Truths of reason and truths of fact, Leibniz pointed out, are quite different.

Leibniz's God, however, knows the reasons for every fact. The world of necessary reasons and the world of contingent facts are all the same to Him. According to Leibniz's principle of sufficient reason, there is a sufficient reason why things are exactly the way they are and are not otherwise. If the proposition that "Dan is the bachelor in the van" is true, then Dan's masculinity as well as his location are both necessary truths, from God's perspective.

Unlike Spinoza's God, which is identical with Nature or Substance, Leibniz's God transcends the world. This God created the world in terms of a set of monads – basic units of psychic force or energy. Each monad mirrors the universe and, unlike matter, is indivisible. Each monad has a psychic life of its own. Some high level monads, in the category of human beings, are free. Freedom for these monads means that they are consciously aware of their inner tendency to actualize their built-in purposes. God, of course, knows how they will realize their freedom. God created a pre-established harmony in the universe of monads and this world is the best of all logically possible worlds.

Leibniz, like Descartes and Spinoza, believed that reason was the key source for real knowledge. He, along with Newton, invented the calculus. Unlike Spinoza, however, Leibniz wanted to maintain the distinctions between God, individual human beings, and nature without fusing all of them in the idea of Substance. This mathematical genius, however, created a very complex metaphysical theory, pluralistic idealism (or panpsychism), based on his rational speculations.

LOCKE

John Locke was the founding father of the British empiricists. Empiricists believe that all knowledge comes from our sensory experiences. They reject the claim, put forward by the rationalists, that knowledge comes primarily from reason or the mind. Empiricists have a hard time dealing with speculative rationalistic metaphysics and the epistemology based on innate (inborn) ideas.

Locke attacked Descartes' belief in "innate ideas" by using "Ockham's razor." "Ockham's razor" is the principle of simplicity, advanced by the medieval philosopher, William of Ockham, according to which simple explanations that account for the facts adequately, are better than needlessly complex explanations. Locke believed that his empiricism was simpler and, therefore, better than Descartes' rationalism as a way to explain knowledge.

Empiricism starts by assuming that the mind, at birth, is a blank slate. On this view, "there is nothing in the mind that was not, at first in the senses." All knowledge can be constructed from "simple ideas" which start off as sensory perceptions. Simple ideas cannot be broken down into more basic ideas. They include perceptions relating to colors, odors, textures, tastes, and noises. Sensations like green, red, sour, hard, rough, smooth, sweet, loud, etc., are the building blocks of knowledge.

Simple ideas may be combined to form "complex ideas." An orange, for example, may be understood by using such simple ideas as "yellow," "spherical," and "sweet" to describe it. By comparing, contrasting, blending, noting relationships, and generalizing, the mind reflects on the data given to it by the senses and generates a wide range of complex ideas. The complex idea of God, for instance, is a blend of simple ideas like duration, knowledge, power, wisdom, and infinity. Abstract concepts, or universals, are simply based on collections of sensory data representing particular things. A concept like "circularity," for Locke, is a "general idea" formed by observing specific circular things. Only particulars are real, from Locke's viewpoint.

To understand reality, according to Locke, we must distinguish between primary and secondary qualities. Primary qualities are those features of external objects that really reside in those objects. They include qualities like extension, size, and shape. Secondary qualities are features that we frequently think of as belonging to external objects but, in fact, exist only in the mind. They include qualities like colors, tastes, and sounds. In understanding the reality of a basketball, for instance, we can all agree on the size and shape of this object. Consequently, we can easily distinguish it from a football, baseball, golf ball, or ping pong ball. In reporting on the color of the basketball, however, we might have some disagreements. Some people might see it as a shade of brown while others may see it as dark orange. This happens, according to Locke's theory, because size is a primary quality while color is a secondary quality of objects.

The mind represents the objects of the external world. This theory of Locke is called representative realism. To claim that the mind duplicates external objects is to subscribe to naïve realism. Locke s version of empiricism, representative realism, seemed to capture our common sense understanding of reality. Nevertheless, it was severely attacked by the empiricist who followed him.

BERKELEY

George Berkeley (1685-1753) was the empiricist who came right after Locke. He was an admirer as well as a critic of Locke's representative realism. Berkeley's version of empiricism is called phenomenalism.

Phenomenalism is the view that knowledge comes to us directly through perception. Whereas Locke believed that our perceptions represent reality, Berkeley held that our perceptions are reality. In Locke's view, the primary qualities of objects, (size, shape, etc.) are in the objects, but the secondary qualities (colors, odors, etc.) are in the mind. Berkeley pointed out, however, that the only way to know these so-called primary qualities is to use our visual and tactile perceptions. To learn about the size of the basketball, for example, we need to see it and touch it. Thus, from Berkeley's point of view, what Locke calls "primary qualities" are really interpretations of secondary qualities; and this implies that they also exist, strictly speaking, in the mind.

To be is to be perceived. A material object is a cluster of perceptions. Perceptions are ideas in the mind. Therefore, a material object is nothing more than a cluster of ideas in the mind.

Let us take the way in which we get to know an apple as an example of this way of looking at things. We get data about the apple by using our five senses: seeing, touching, tasting, smelling, and hearing. Seeing the apple gives us visual data. Touching the apple gives us tactile data. Tasting the apple gives us gustatory data. Smelling the apple gives us olfactory data. Hearing the apple gives us auditory data. If we now list our perceptual data, we hit upon descriptions such as the following: red, spherical, sweet, crisp, crunchy, etc. If we ask about the meaning of a term like "red", Berkeley would say that this perception, like all of the others, refers to an idea in the mind. The apple itself is nothing more than a bundle of perceptions in the mind. Other clusters of perceptions we call "oranges," "clocks," "tables," etc. To use the sensory data from our direct perception in describing an object is to get to know the object.

Unperceived material objects do not exist. The universe contains perceptions, which are ideas, and the entities which have these ideas, namely, spirits. Does this mean that a material object which is not perceived, simply vanishes? Not at all, Berkeley believed that God, the universal spirit, perceives all things.

Bishop Berkeley's pluralistic idealism stands in sharp contrast to Hobbes' materialism. For Hobbes, ideas are nothing but physical motions in the brain. For Berkeley, objects are nothing but clusters of ideas in the mind.

HUME

David Hume was the British empiricist who came after Berkeley. He used his epistemological fork to pick up a huge chunk of skepticism, which some philosophers, notably Kant, found impossible to swallow.

Hume's epistemological fork is the idea that all true propositions must either be analytic or synthetic. As we recall from Leibniz's work, analytic propositions are true by logical definition and synthetic propositions are true by factual confirmation. Hume calls analytic propositions "relations of ideas" and synthetic propositions "matters of fact." A typical analytic proposition is "Bachelors are unmarried males," and a typical synthetic proposition is "Bachelors are frequently messy."

There are a number of key differences between analytic statements and synthetic statements. Since they are true by definition, analytic propositions are necessarily true. To deny an analytic proposition is to involve oneself in a self-contradiction. To claim that John is a "married bachelor," for instance, is to contradict oneself. Analytic propositions are known a priori (before experience) to be true. Synthetic propositions, on the other hand, are not true by definition and are not necessarily always true. To deny a synthetic proposition is not to involve oneself in a contradiction. To claim, "the bachelors on our campus are neat," is not to contradict oneself. Synthetic propositions are known a posteriori (after experience) to be true.

Hume believed that the existence of a priori analytic propositions shows that there are necessary truths. These necessary truths, however, are merely definitions. They are certain but empty, in the sense that they do not tell us anything about the world. Analytic truths are merely verbal truths. Synthetic truths, on the other hand, are informative but uncertain. They tell us about the facts of the world, but they must be confirmed by experience. Thus, rationalists who want to know about the world, prior to experience, are misguided. Synthetic propositions are known a posteriori (after experience).

Sensory experience is the basis for all factual knowledge. This, of course, is the view that is shared by all empiricists. Hume attempted to apply empiricism in a very rigorous manner. He did this by insisting that all knowledge begins with perceptions. Perceptions come to us as impressions. Whereas our original impressions are "lively," our ideas are obtained when we reflect upon these impressions. The mind is capable of compounding, transposing or diminishing the perceptions that it gets from the senses. Our imagination, for instance, can come up with things like "unicorns" or golden beaches. It is not hard, however, to see the original impressions that the mind blended to create these creative concepts.

But what about basic ideas like "God," "the self," and "the cause-effect relationship"? How do we account for these ideas? For Hume, the idea of God came from the impressions of wisdom and goodness that we observed in human beings and stretched to infinity. The idea of "the self" as an unchanging substance is without any basis, because there is no impression that could serve as the foundation for this idea. Hume's analysis of this concept yielded impressions like heat or cold, love or hatred, and pain or pleasure. There is no impression corresponding to continuous self-identity. Thus, although memory makes us think of the existence of a "self," careful analysis forced Hume to question this concept. A similar approach forced Hume to question "the cause-effect relationship."

Causality, the cause-effect relationship, is the basis for science. Can we find the basic impressions, or sense data, to serve as the foundation for this critical concept? Let us use Hume's example to illustrate a very clear case of cause and effect. If ball (x) hits ball (y) and y moves, we are inclined to think that x's movement caused y's movement. But what exactly can we observe? We perceive x moving before y moving (priority). We perceive x touching y (contiguity). We do not, however, observe necessary connection. This feature of "causality" is never perceived. It is psychological expectation rather than any factual validation that makes us believe in causality.

Skepticism regarding causality has wide ranging implications, however. How do we know that the future will resemble the past? How do we know that the natural laws will be the same tomorrow? If there are no necessary connections between physical events, how do we know that bread, which nourished us today, will not poison us tomorrow? Skepticism regarding causality puts all of our scientific knowledge and common sense knowledge in jeopardy.

KANT

Immanuel Kant's critical philosophy was designed to rescue philosophy from Hume's skepticism. In order to do this, he tried to reconcile empiricism and rationalism. In order to summarize the key distinctions between these two theories of knowledge, let us examine the following chart:

Rationalism	Empiricism
Descartes	Locke
mind	senses
innate ideas	no innate ideas
abstract conceptions	concrete perceptions
deduction	induction
universal	particulars
General Organizing Principles	Data of Experienced Materials

Kant's strategy was to synthesize or connect the conflicting viewpoints of empiricism and rationalism. For Kant, sensory perceptions without mental conceptions are blind. On the other hand, conceptions without perceptions are empty. Knowledge, on the Kantian view, must be seen as a happy marriage between conceptions and perceptions. By emphasizing perceptions, Kant partly agreed with the empiricists. On the other hand, by focusing on conceptions he also agreed with the rationalists. Even though knowledge begins with sensory perceptions, it does not follow that knowledge arises from perceptions. The human mind, Kant believed, is active in the construction of knowledge because it contains a system of categories which is constantly processing the raw data of our sensory experiences.

Our knowledge starts with perceptions. Our perceptions give us a wide range of sensory data. Data are perceived with regard to space and time. Space and time are not features of the external world, like dogs and cats, but necessary features in the structure of the human mind. Space and time are the "permanent eye-glasses," so to speak, through which we see all of the events in the external world.

The mind's category system allows us to understand the world. This, in effect, was Kant's Copernican Revolution in philosophy. Just as Copernicus substituted the sun for the earth as the center of our universe, Kant substituted the mind's category system for the senses' data as the central factor in our search for knowledge. The active mind blends and unifies our sensory experiences by means of the following categories: quantity, quality, relation, and modality. Quantity deals with unity, plurality, or totality. Quality deals with affirmation, negation, or limitation. Relation deals with substance, causality, or community. Modality deals with possibility vs. impossibility, existence vs. non-existence, or necessity vs. contingency. With respect to quantity, the mind makes judgments about one or many items. With respect to quality, the mind makes judgments that are either positive affirmations or negations. With regard to relation, the mind makes judgments about cause-effect relationships or substance-accident relationships. With respect to modality, the mind makes judgments about impossibility or possibility and necessity or contingency. Out of a multiplicity of sensory data, the category system of the mind imposes orderly consistent patterns on our experiences.

Kant believed he could answer Hume's skepticism by appealing to the centrality of the mind's category system. Hume believed we could never have knowledge of the world a priori (before experience) because our sensory data, which give us our so-called knowledge, is really a set of disconnected impressions in which nothing is logically necessary and anything is possible. Kant, however, argued that the mind unifies our experience with relational concepts like "substance" and "causality," for examples. The mind recognizes and organizes clusters of sense data as substances. Sensory data that the mind interprets as red, round, crunchy, and sweet get classified together as constituting an apple, for instance. By means of the categories, we understand that there is a universal and necessary connection between a cause and its effect. This means that the mind's structure allows us to have knowledge of the world that cannot be falsified by any experience. The mind's structure, in other words, allows us to have synthetic a priori knowledge.

Let us review our relevant distinctions to understand Kant's idea that the mind's categories give us knowledge. The following chart should help us to visualize the distinctions between analytic and synthetic propositions and a posteriori and a priori judgments:

	ANALYTIC (Relations of Ideas)	SYNTHETIC (Matters of Fact)
A Posteriori (after experience)		1. Bachelors are frequently messy. 2. Palm Beach widows are rich.
A Priori (before experience)	1. Bachelors are unmarried males. 2. Widows have dead spouses.	1. Objects exist in space and time. 2. Every event has a cause.

Kant tried to show that the mind's structure gives us real knowledge about the world. If our car fails to start, for instance, we know that there has to be a cause to explain this unfortunate event. This knowledge comes from our sensory perceptions as they are organized and classified by the mind's concept of causality. This is why, unlike the empiricists, Kant held that synthetic a priori knowledge existed. Thus, we do not need to swallow Hume's skepticism about our knowledge of events in the world.

Kant was somewhat skeptical about our knowledge of things that went beyond any sense experience, however. Metaphysical concepts, like God, the soul, and the free will, are not based on sensory perceptions. Thus, they belong to the realm of moral faith rather than the realm of knowledge. The realm of faith is called the noumenal world and the realm of knowledge is called the phenomenal world. Our knowledge is restricted to things as they are perceived by the senses and organized, classified, categorized, and conceptualized by the structure of the mind. God, the soul, and the free will, however, are necessary assumptions for a practical, moral faith, if not, strictly speaking, objects of knowledge. Kant's theory of reality may be summarized as follows:

NOUMENA (FAITH): thing-in-itself

PHENOMENA (KNOWLEDGE): thing- as perceived and categorized

HEGEL

Georg Wilhelm Friedrich Hegel (1770-1831) agreed with Kant's emphasis on the mind's structure as the key to knowledge. He had problems, however, with the notion that there is a noumenal world which must forever remain unknown. According to Hegel's view, everything can be known because the structure of mind is the structure of reality.

In order to develop this idea, let us explore Hegel's theory of reality, namely, absolute idealism. Hegel's absolute idealism begins with the proposition that the ultimate reality is Absolute Mind, or Spirit, or God. The Absolute is that which is completely self-contained because it does not need anything else. Everything that exists is a manifestation of this Reality-As-A-Whole. The Absolute Spirit, or Mind, or God, is manifested in a material form as Nature. Nature is spirit materialized. The Absolute Mind, or Spirit, or God is also manifested in a conceptual form as Logic. Logic is spirit conceptualized. Furthermore, the Absolute Spirit has a purely objective manifestation (objective mind) and a purely subjective manifestation (subjective mind). The purpose of Hegel's philosophy is to get a systematic understanding of reality as a whole. In his view, nothing can be understood in isolation. Every particular thing and every particular truth can only be understood as a part of the totality of things and truths. To illustrate this comprehensive view, let us examine the following diagram:

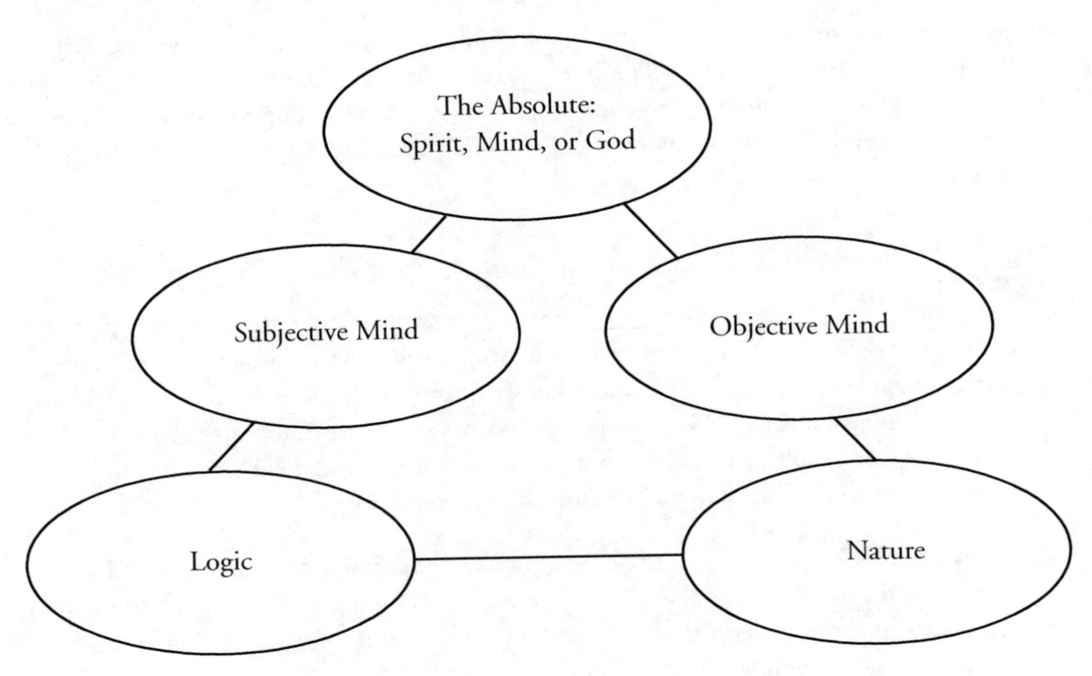

The ultimate reality is The Absolute Mind, or Spirit, or God. Spirit is the synthesis of Logic and Nature. Logic deals with the structure of ideas. Nature deals with the physical and organic sciences. Subjective Mind deals with the individual's mind and is studied, for example, in psychology. Objective Mind deals with legal, moral, and social reality and is studied in the social sciences. Absolute Mind, reality at the highest level, is a synthesis of Subjective Mind and Objective Mind. Absolute Mind or Spirit is revealed in art, religion, and philosophy. In art, the Absolute Spirit manifests itself in terms of sensuous forms. In religion, The Absolute Spirit is represented in imagery and figurative language. In philosophy, The Absolute Spirit is understood as pure thought or pure Universal Reason. Thus, every subject reveals a partial aspect of reality and it is the philosopher's job to explain the nature of reality as an integrated whole.

Hegel understands everything and every truth in terms of a series of triads: thesis – antithesis – synthesis. According to his dialectical logic, a thesis (representing an idea) can only be understood in terms of its opposite (an antithesis). Each idea, by itself, is inadequate and in tension with another. This tension is resolved by a synthesis which includes the best aspects of each partial idea. This dynamic logic of thesis – antithesis – synthesis accounts for all reality as well as the developments in the ongoing process of history. Dialectical reason continues on indefinitely and reveals the progressive unfolding of history and reality.

Hegel's theory of reality is called absolute idealism, in contrast to the subjective idealism of Berkeley. His theory of knowledge is rationalism. Taken together, these theories had a mesmerizing effect on philosophers since they indicate that everything is interrelated in the historic process and every truth has a part to play in an elaborate, logically coherent system of truth, seen as an integrated whole.

DEWEY

John Dewey (1859-1952) was, and probably still is, the most famous representative of American pragmatism. Early in his career he was greatly influenced by the comprehensive organic developmental perspective of Hegel's idealism. Like Kant, Dewey also believed that the mind did not merely mirror the world in a passive manner. But Darwin's evolutionary theory had the most impact on his thoughts about reality and knowledge.

For Dewey, biological evolution is the basis for our intellectual life. Thinking is really about trying to solve the problems of adjusting to the natural and social world. Just as evolution never reaches a state of absolute perfection, our thinking must continuously reconstruct our ideas to keep pace with a constantly changing world.

Dewey's theory of knowledge is called "instrumentalism." According to this pragmatic concept, ideas are tools for solving problems. All thinking involves encountering a problem, entertaining hypotheses, formulating plans of action, making observations, testing facts, and trying to resolve the problem. Inquiry is a continuous process. We are constantly trying to adjust to our environment or to change the environment to meet human needs and interests. An idea or a theory may be considered "true" if it works by allowing us to act successfully in this constantly changing world. Thus, thinking is not a search for "absolute truth," but an activity geared toward solving personal and social problems. Pragmatic intelligence is needed to achieve a satisfying relationship with our environment.

Dewey's naturalism stands in sharp contrast to idealistic metaphysics. Like religious cults, Dewey thinks that idealistic metaphysical beliefs are designed to escape from the uncomfortable changes in life. From this perspective, the search for absolutely certain, fixed, immutable, universal, eternal truth is misguided. Knowledge is really about dealing intelligently with a constantly changing natural and social world.

Dewey's pragmatism had a profound impact on our educational system. Pragmatism in philosophy is associated with the progressive movement in education. Whereas traditional education favored authoritarian relationships in the school, along with techniques of rote learning, the progressive movement emphasized democratic relationships and practical experiential learning. The idea that we "learn by doing," in a cooperative manner, is one of the implications of this experimental pragmatic view of knowledge. For Dewey, knowing was always about problem solving.

RUSSELL

Bertrand Russell (1872-1970) was an English philosopher who started off as an idealist in metaphysics but ended up as one of the founding fathers of analytic philosophy. He helped to develop a theory of reality that we associate with this movement, namely, logical atomism.

Logical atomism is the view that the world is made up of a number of basic facts. Each simple fact is independent of all the other atomic facts and could remain the same even if the related facts were different. This is very different from Hegel's view that an object's relationship to other objects constituted a part of its essential nature and, ultimately, only one reality existed – The Absolute. Russell's view is based on the idea of a pluralistic universe, with many separate things. The properties and relations of things are facts. Complex molecular facts may be broken down into basic atomic facts.

The primary function of language is to represent facts. Propositions may be true or false insofar as they correspond with facts. On this view, truth is not a feature of the world, like a cat or a dog. Neither is it an internal feature of propositions. Truth is rather a correspondence between a proposition and a fact. This idea of truth is called the correspondence theory of truth.

At this juncture, it is in order to contrast the various views of truth along with their associated theories of knowledge, as developed by representative philosophers.

Representative Philosophers	Knowledge Theories	Truth Theories	Short Definitions
(1) Hegel	rationalism	coherence	A consistent belief system
(2) Dewey	pragmatism	pragmatic	A guide to successful action
(3) Russell	empiricism	correspondence	A connection between a proposition and a fact

Logical atomism had a great impact on a group of philosophers who were trained in mathematics and science. In their quest to provide a scientific foundation for philosophy, they restricted all meaningful statements to two classes of propositions: ANALYTIC and SYNTHETIC. Analytic propositions include those that are true by definition. "A rainy day is a wet day" would be an example of an analytic proposition. Synthetic propositions are true by verification. "Today is a wet day in our city" would be an example of a synthetic statement. Synthetic propositions deal with the way the world is, while analytic propositions deal with the concepts in our language. A statement which was neither analytic nor synthetic would be, strictly speaking, "non-sense." To say that "Mary's car stopped due to fate" would be an example of a "non-sense" statement, insofar as it is neither a truth of reason nor a truth of fact. All meaningful statements must be logically consistent or scientifically verifiable. This verification theory of meaning became the cornerstone of a school of thought called logical positivism.

The logical positivists had a great deal of respect for logic, mathematics, and the sciences. They were very skeptical, however, of the idea of metaphysical truth. To claim, for instance, that "The Absolute is the sovereign of the universe" is to make a claim that cannot be verified by any sensory data. Thus, it must be seen as "non-sense," according to this school of thought.

WITTGENSTEIN

Ludwig Wittgenstein (1889-1951) was a student and a colleague of Russell. In his early years, he was famous for connecting Russell's logical atomism with logical positivism. He believed that language could be reduced to a set of basic propositions, which would correspond with observable atomic facts or states of affairs. According to his "picture theory of language," the function of a proposition is to describe a specific state of affairs in the world.

How can we know what exists in the world? Wittgenstein, like Russell, early in his career accepted the theory of phenomenalism. According to Phenomenalism, the basic minimum that we must suppose to exist, are sense data. The objects of common sense (tables and chairs) as well as the objects in our scientific theories (atoms, electrons) are definable In terms of sense data. Sense data, the data of our immediate sensory experience, are what we truly know. Common sense objects and scientific entities seem to make sense if we claim that, at least in principle, they can be reduced to our awarenesses, or sensory data. Sense data, therefore, seemed to provide the absolutely certain foundation for knowledge of the world. Phenomenalism seemed to give us a theory of knowledge resting on solid verifiable data.

But should we base all knowledge on sense data as the phenomenalists believed? Later in his career, Wittgenstein challenged this idea by his famous "private language" argument. It may be summarized as follows: If phenomenalism is true, then all knowledge, including the knowledge of language, must rest on sensory data. If this is true, then a "private language" could be logically possible since different people might have different sensory data. The concept of a "private language," however, is absurd since language is a set of symbols with publicly shared rules. Thus, phenomenalism is false.

Wittgenstein's anti-phenomenalism set the stage for "the linguistic turn" in philosophy. Instead of thinking that language serves primarily to describe facts in the world, it was now seen in a flexible way. Language was viewed as a set of tools. It can serve many functions in many contexts – science, religion, work, play, etc. Like playing a game, using a language is a rule-governed social activity. The job of the philosopher is to understand the "language games" in use, in a wide range of fields. These ideas of Wittgenstein set the stage for philosophers to practice "ordinary language analysis" and "conceptual analysis," in order to make sense of the logical geography of our ideas as they are used in a wide variety of meaningful contexts.

RORTY

Richard Rorty (1931-) challenged the idea of universal objective truth by attacking the idea of "representationalism." Representationalism is the view that true beliefs accurately represent reality. True beliefs are supposed to correspond to states of affairs as they exist objectively in the world. In this account of knowledge, the mind is like a mirror which portrays the objective truths of the world when it is functioning properly.

According to Rorty, however, our minds, bodies, and language have been shaped by our natural environment and culture. There is therefore no mind – independent reality to which our true beliefs must correspond in order to count as knowledge. What counts as knowledge is based on the standards of evidence which are employed in a particular culture. Rorty's anti-representationalism means that there is no pure universal objective truth. Plato sought truth in a world of pure ideal forms. St. Augustine sought truth in the soul. Descartes sought truth by doubting everything so as to find absolute certainty. Kant sought truth by examining the mind's category system. But Rorty believes that our ideas of truth are based on the contingent standards of our community or culture. Truth is whatever survives all objections within our culturally-based conversations.

To illustrate Rorty's anti-representationalism, according to which there is no pure universal objective truth about the world, let us explore a specific example. In our elementary schools we learn that "Columbus discovered America in 1492." This "truth," however, is loaded with cultural assumptions. It reflects a European cultural perspective and downplays the perspective of native Americans. Thus, it illustrates Rorty's concern about the ways in which our cultural perspective shapes our perceptions of reality and knowledge.

QUINE

Willard Van Orman Quine (1908-2000) was an analytical philosopher who recommended a pragmatic view of truth. He attacked the notion of foundationalism in epistemology. Foundationalism is the view that a belief counts as knowledge if and only if it is logically tied to propositions that are absolutely certain (incorrigible). In order to illustrate foundationalism, let us examine the following diagram:

b
bbb
bbbb
bbbbbb
bbbbbbb
BBBB

Traditional philosophers have tended to favor foundationalism. They have argued about what constitutes the foundation for knowledge but have agreed that some rock-solid foundation is necessary. Should the foundation be religious dogmas, innate ideas, mental categories, or sense data? Different theorists have put forward different sources to serve as the basis for knowledge.

Quine's anti-foundationalism, however, challenged this "building" model of knowledge. Instead of thinking of beliefs as bricks in a building needing to rest on an absolutely solid foundation of certainty, we should think of our beliefs as parts of a web of beliefs. Let us explore the following picture:

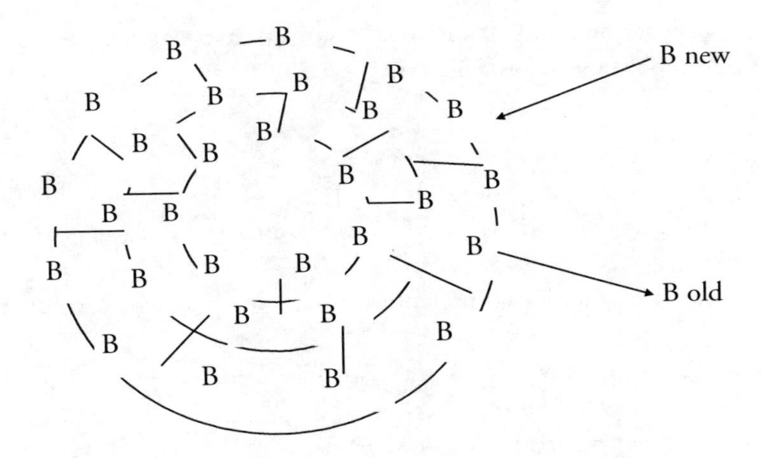

Quine's theory assumes that knowledge does not require absolutely certain foundational beliefs. Our true beliefs should automatically count as knowledge if they allow us to experience the world successfully and are logically consistent. Every belief, however, is capable of being revised if our web breaks down. In revising a belief, to ensure logical consistency, we have to revise the interconnected beliefs in the web of beliefs. Peripheral beliefs require minor revisions. Central beliefs require extensive revisions. But no belief is immune from revisions. The continuous reinterpretations of beliefs is necessary so as to keep pace with changing realities.

Quine's anti-foundationalist view reminds us of the concerns of pragmatic philosophers. The tendency to focus on the ways in which beliefs are acquired and revised has encouraged epistemologists to explore psychology. Should we embrace a "naturalized epistemology" and think of this area of philosophy as simply a part of psychology? Many philosophers would not want to go this far. Questions regarding the justification of beliefs still need to be examined. Nevertheless, few would deny that scientists and philosophers should continue to enlighten us about the processes and criteria for knowledge.

REVIEW QUESTIONS

(Short Answers)

1. What are the basic questions in metaphysics and epistemology?
2. Are universal concepts more real than particular things?
3. How are "spirit" and "matter" related?
4. Does a non-physical "mind" exist?
5. Is reality basically one substance?
6. Is there certainty in knowledge?
7. Must knowledge be based on a foundation of absolute certainty?
8. Does purely objective knowledge exist?

(Long Answers)

1. Do the concepts of "God," "free will," and "immortality" have a basis in reality or are they illusions?
2. Should we think of reality as different manifestations of one basic substance? Why? Why not?
3. Are most claims to knowledge distorted by bias? Why? Why not?
4. What are the best tests for truth?
5. What are the best criteria for knowledge?

chapter 5

Philosophy of Religion

The philosophy of religion is one of the ways in which philosophy may be applied in other fields of study. There is a philosophy of just about any field that we can imagine: art, science, history, language, law, etc. In every case, philosophy seeks to reveal the meanings of the basic ideas in each form of consciousness and in each universe of discourse. Each field of inquiry carries with it its specific concepts that define it as a special realm of meaning. The philosopher's job is to examine the assumptions and implications of these distinctive concepts. In the field of religion, there are a number of key ideas to explore: the nature and existence of God, the immortality of the soul, the possibility of miracles, the intelligibility of religious language as factual propositions, or metaphorical descriptions, etc.

Perhaps the most basic questions have to do with the nature and existence of God. Both questions involve a great deal of controversy. With respect to the nature of God, we have to deal with the phenomenon of religious diversity. There are many religious groups throughout history, that have some idea of a god or gods. Polytheism and monotheism come with many variations in belief systems. There are many different ideas of the ultimate reality, or God, in the world's religions. In Hinduism, the ultimate deity is Brahma. In Taoism, the Tao is the final reality. In Judaism, the ultimate reality is "The Holy One." In Islam, Allah is the title for God. In Christianity, "The Holy Trinity" is the idea of God. What complicates matters is that within each religion there are a variety of groups. There are different kinds of Hindus, Muslims, Jews, and Christians, for examples.

In the history of philosophy there is also a good deal of diversity regarding the idea of a deity. Plato's "Demiurge," Aristotle's "Fist Mover," the Stoic's "Logos," Plotinus' "The One," Descartes' "Infinite Perfection." Spinoza's "Substance" and Hegel's "Absolute Spirit" are some of the concepts of a deity that we encounter. Given the multiplicity of religious groups and the variety of philosophical ideas, is there any way to find the generic essence of a possible deity?

If we are in search of the general criteria for a possible deity, a few features might come to mind. If God is assumed to be personal, attributes such as omniscience, omnipotence, omnibenevolence, and omnipresence might be seen as essential characteristics of this ultimate reality. That is to say, the supreme being has to be all-knowing, all-powerful, all-good, and always present, respectively. A being could not be the supreme being if ignorance, metaphysical impotence, and evil, for examples, were features of this reality. If there is a God, then ultimate knowledge, power, and goodness would have to be some of the necessary "divine features," or so it would seem.

This, to be sure, does not prove that there is a God. It is possible to know the essence of something even if the thing does not exist. A unicorn, to use the standard example, has an essence but does not have an existence. We know that the essence of a unicorn is to be a horse and to have one horn. If someone claimed that she saw a beautiful unicorn at the zoo last summer, however, we would certainly be amused because we would still realize that unicorns do not exist. Is God like the unicorn? Does God have a fabulous essence without any existence?

There are three major philosophical perspectives on this issue, namely, theism, agnosticism, and atheism. Theists believe that there is a god. Agnostics believe that we can never know if there is or isn't a god. Atheists believe that there is no god at all. Are there good arguments to prove or deny the existence of God? This is the central question in the philosophy of religion.

Many people believe in the existence of a God because of some authority. For them, authority is the ultimate source of knowledge. Authorities might include religious leaders, parents, peers, etc. Appealing to the authority of the sacred literature, within a particular religious tradition, is another way to use what is taken to be an authoritative source. With respect to this appeal to sacred scriptures, mystics, prophets, and apostles, for examples, are assumed to have a sort of privileged access to the realm of the divine. Thus, their writings are seen as authoritative sources in their communities of faith.

What is the relationship between faith and reason? Can the existence of God be proved by reason? Is it merely a dogma (an unquestioned belief) that is supported by faith? Is it better to have faith or not to have faith in the existence of God? These questions inspire and/or provoke a good deal of argumentation in the history of philosophical thought.

ST. ANSELM

St. Anselm (1033-1109) was one of the first to employ a purely philosophical outlook in investigating the existence of God. That is to say, in seeking to prove the existence of God, he did not start off by assuming what he intended to prove. Although on a psychological level he did not doubt the existence of God, on a logical level he did not rely on exclusively religious assumptions to construct his argument for God's existence.

The famous argument that he came up with is called "the ontological argument," based on reason. The argument is as follows: The concept of God is "a being than which nothing greater can be conceived." In other words, God is the greatest conceivable being. Even an atheist who denies God's existence, understands what is being denied, insofar as the atheist knows the meaning of the concept of God. For the atheist, God merely exits in the understanding but not in reality. But to exist in the understanding and in reality is greater than to exist only in the understanding. To exist is greater than not to exist. Therefore, by logical implication, God must exist.

The most famous objection to the ontological argument came from a monk named Gaunilo. He argued that, based on St. Anselm's reasoning, "the most perfect island" must exist. Since it would be more perfect to exist than not to exist, the most perfect island must necessarily exit. Anselm, however, believed that this sort of argument could only work in the case of God, since ultimate greatness, or perfection, is only tied to the essence of God. To use other examples, as in the case of Gaunilo's illustration, would lead to absurdity. God alone is essentially perfect and this implies God's existence.

Philosophers have been scratching their heads over this short argument for almost a thousand years. Some see it as merely a clever but illegitimate attempt to derive "existence" from "essence." On the other hand, some see it as a brilliant attempt to prove God's existence based on nothing but reason. At any rate, this ontological argument is one of the classic arguments that is attacked and reformulated, in many ways, throughout the history of the philosophy of religion.

ST. THOMAS AQUINAS

Another set of classic arguments in this field, was set forth by St. Thomas Aquinas. Whereas St. Anselm relied on reason to formulate his ontological argument, Aquinas relied on experience as the basis for his attempt to prove the existence of God. He believed that there are "Five Ways" to prove God's existence. The first three ways are variations of the cosmological argument. The fourth way is a type of moral argument and the fifth way is a teleological (design) argument.

Let us examine Aquinas's Five Ways by starting with his cosmological arguments. The first argument hinges on the nature of motion in the world. Things that move require something to put them in motion. If everything required another moving thing to put it in motion, there would be no first mover. If there is no first mover, then nothing would be in motion. Since things are in motion, a first mover must exist which is not moved by anything else. This unmoved mover is God. The first way, the argument from motion, is sometimes interpreted in a very general way, as focusing on the idea of change. Thus, the unmoved mover is seen as the source of all change in the universe.

The second argument for the existence of God turns on the idea of cause and effect. In the world of our sensory perceptions, everything is caused by something. Nothing can serve as its own cause. Now, if everything requires a cause, in an absolute sense, then there would be no first cause. If no first cause existed then there would be no first effect. This would imply that no second, third or fourth effect, etc., would exist. To put forward the existence of an uncaused first cause is to affirm the existence of God.

The third cosmological argument for God's existence is a little tricky. It hinges on the distinction between necessary and contingent beings. Contingent beings need not exist and eventually will go out of existence. Now just about anything that we can think of – dogs, cats, chairs, tables, etc. – exist contingently. Dogs need not exist, in the sense that we can imagine a universe without them. Even your favorite dog does not exist necessarily. Things that exist contingently, at some time, did not exist and, at some point in time, will go out of existence. But everything could not exist contingently since that would mean that at one time nothing existed, at least this would be a logical possibility. However, if nothingness ever existed, then, even now, it would be impossible for anything to exist. Thus, there must be a necessary (non-contingent) being. But what if the necessity of this necessary being came from another being? And this being's necessity came from another being? Aquinas believed that in order to stop an infinite regress in necessary beings, we must assume that there is a necessary being that has its own necessity built into itself. This ultimately necessary being is God.

The fourth argument for God's existence is a type of moral argument. This argument is based on the idea of degrees of perfection in things. We constantly make judgments based on the degree of excellence, nobility, truth, beauty, and goodness in things. For example, we think in terms like "good," "better," and "best." This illustrates that we are aware of varying degrees of perfection. Thus, there must be a source of these perfections: perfect goodness, perfect truth, perfect beauty, etc. This ultimate source of perfection, which is implicit in our value judgments and in comparison to which everything else must be seen as relatively imperfect, is God.

The fifth argument for God's existence is called the teleological argument. It hinges on the idea that things in nature act for a purpose or an end. Natural things function according to a design or a plan. This implies that nature provides us with evidence for a divine designer who directs things to fulfill their purpose. Nature's divine architect is God.

At this point, we have explored all of the classic arguments for the existence of God. St. Anselm's ontological argument is based on examining the idea of God. St. Thomas Aquinas' cosmological argument hinges on making inferences from our experiences of the world, as in his first three ways of trying to prove God's existence. Aquinas' fourth argument is a type of moral argument and his fifth argument, the design argument, is called the teleological argument. These four classic arguments are attacked and reformulated in a variety of ways in the history of the philosophy of religion.

JULIAN OF NORWICH

Julian, or Juliana, of Norwich (1342-1414) set forth a mystical approach to exploring the existence of God. Mystics tend to believe that a direct inner illumination provides us with knowledge concerning the realm of the divine. In Juliana's case, these revelatory experiences were called "showings." Her "showings" disclosed that God loves us as a parent and nurtures us in our development.

Mystical visions, of course, are not the same as rational conceptions. But they need not contradict the ideas of reason. Juliana also believed that anyone could have these sorts of mystical intuitions. These revelations were not restricted to special religious leaders because this would limit God's power to communicate divine truths. God could reveal these truths to anyone who was open and receptive to them.

There is, however, a limit to the value of mystical visions. The beliefs which stem from these powerful experiences of inner illumination might seem to be illusions, delusions, or even hallucinations to people outside of the religious tradition which inspired the mystics. Whereas some mystics might be content with their experiences and might think of evaluating theistic, agnostic, and atheistic arguments as trivial academic exercises, most philosophers, in pursuit of communicable truth, see no alternative to constructing and assessing arguments.

DESCARTES

Descartes, the famous rationalistic philosopher and mathematician, set forth three important arguments in the philosophy of religion. These arguments were creative reconstructions of some of the classic arguments, with the first two being rather similar.

Descartes' first argument was based on the idea of God coupled with the concept of cause and effect. It was thus a combination of ontological and cosmological viewpoints. It ran as follows:

My mind has an idea of God as an infinite and perfect being. There must be a cause for this idea. To explain any effect, the cause itself has to be at least as great. I am not the cause since I am not perfect. Nothingness is not the cause since nothing comes from nothing. Therefore, God must be the cause of the idea of God.

Descartes' second argument focused on the idea that God must be the cause of Descartes himself and not simply Descartes' idea of God. It may be summarized as follows: I am someone who has an idea of God. Everything in existence has a cause that allows it to exist and sustains its existence. The only being that is adequate to cause and sustain me is God. Therefore, God exists.

Descartes' third argument, a variation on the ontological argument, was quite different from his first two proofs. It may be summarized in the following way: My concept of God is of a being who has all of the perfections. Existence is a perfection. This implies that it is logically impossible to think of God as not existing. Therefore God exists.

Like St. Anselm, Descartes thought that the ontological argument was totally conclusive. He offered an analogous argument to support this notion. It ran as follows: I have a concept of a triangle in my mind. This idea is of a figure with 180 degrees. A figure with 180 degrees has two times 90 degrees. Therefore a triangle has two times 90 degrees.

If the ontological argument works, it would imply that reason alone could prove the existence of God. Whereas Anselm and Descartes held this view, it was subjected to intense criticism by Kant, as we will see later on.

PASCAL

Blaise Pascal (1623-1662) was a French scientist and mathematician. Late in his short life, he developed an interest in the philosophy of religion. Whereas early in his life he worked on mathematical problems and created a calculating machine, later in life he was primarily focused on articulating a religious understanding of human existence.

He also developed a famous argument in the philosophy of religion, which we refer to as "Pascal's Wager." Pascal's Wager contained the following premises: Either God exists or He does not exist. If God exists and we live with this assumption in mind, we might gain happiness and eternal life. If God does not exist, we would lose little if we lived as if He did exist. On the other hand, if God really exists, and we live as atheists, we risk losing everything in eternity. Thus, in using a risk-reward analysis, the belief in God is a relatively safe bet or a prudent wager.

LEIBNIZ

Leibniz, another famous mathematician, also tried to prove the existence of God. He relied on his famous principle of sufficient reason to do this. According to this principle, things are exactly as they are because of a sufficient set of reasons.

Let us illustrate this generic principle with a specific example. Suppose we want to explain any particular phenomenon, say, for instance, a basketball team getting a young superstar. To explain this phenomenon we might put forward, as a partial reason, the fact that the team did very poorly the year before and, consequently, got a first pick in the draft of new players. This, of course, raises the question as to why the team did so poorly the year before. To answer that question would require another set of reasons: the team's chemistry was not good, a key player got injured, the coach's strategy was not intelligent, etc. To explain each of these reasons would require another set of reasons, and these, in turn, would require further reasons. In the nature of professional basketball, the major reasons will tend to involve the coach and, eventually, the general manager and owner of the team. But the nature of rationality is such that it seeks reasons beyond all preliminary and partial reasons. To find an ultimate, complete and final reason is to be forced to go outside the set of incomplete partial reasons to discover the sufficient reason. God alone is a sufficient reason for God's existence. Thus, this principle of sufficient reason leads us from preliminary reasons, to penultimate reasons, to an ultimately sufficient reason, namely, God.

This Leibnizian argument is another variation on the cosmological argument. Many philosophers think of it as another version of Aquinas' third way, which takes us from contingent beings to an ultimately necessary being whose necessity is internally derived. In both cases, God is the ultimately necessary and sufficient Being.

Leibniz also tackled another major problem in the philosophy of religion, namely, the problem of evil. This problem arises when we try to reconcile the evils in the world – murder, terrorism, rape, racism, poverty, hunger, sickness, earthquakes, hurricanes, etc. – with the existence of a God who is all-powerful, all-good, and all-knowing. The problem would vanish if we were to deny any one of these characteristics. For example, we might believe that due to a lack of power, God could not prevent some evils in the world. We might also think that, due to a character flaw, God is not good enough to be bothered by some of the evils in the world. Furthermore, we could get the idea that, due to partial ignorance, God simply does not know about some of the evils in the world. These possible solutions to the problem of evil, however, would distort the traditional concept of God, since they would change essential features in the very definition of God.

Can the idea of divine omnipotence, omni-benevolence, and omniscience be reconciled with the many evils in the world? Leibniz's answer to this question rests on a few distinctions between different kinds of evil – metaphysical, physical, and moral. In a metaphysical sense, evil is imperfection. In a physical sense, evil is suffering, and in a moral sense, evil is sin. Metaphysical evil cannot be avoided because imperfection is a part of the nature of every finite (or limited) thing. Physical evil, or suffering, from a very comprehensive perspective, can lead to a greater good. Suffering sometimes builds character and sometimes, in the long run, it creates the conditions for a better set of circumstances to exist. Moral evil comes as a result of the misuse of our free will. This means that God cannot be blamed for moral evils. In fact, Leibniz believed that the final solution to the problem of evil is to think of the world as "the best of all possible worlds." On this view, it would be logically impossible to have a perfect world with human beings, along with their associated free will, inhabiting it. Thus, even though there are evils in the world, God's omniscience allowed Him to survey all the logical possibilities; His omni-benevolence allowed Him to will the best logical possibility and His omnipotence allowed Him to create the best logical possibility. This means that our world is the best of all logically possible worlds.

Leibniz's concept of "the best of all possible worlds" was an idea that was embraced by some and criticized by others. Alexander Pope, the famous neoclassical poet, wrote a poem entitled, "Essay On Man," in order to justify the ways of God to man and confirm this conclusion of Leibniz. On the other hand, Voltaire, the famous French social critic, wrote a play entitled, Candide, in order to criticize the evils in the world. Thus, Leibniz's philosophical solution to the problem of evil elicited admiration as well as controversy.

HUME

David Hume was one of the most famous skeptics in the philosophy of religion. He focused his skepticism on the cosmological and teleological arguments. In examining both arguments, he questioned the legitimacy of our inferences about the realm of the divine based on our observations of the world.

With regard to the teleological argument, Hume restated it and subjected it to harsh criticisms. According to Hume's restatement, the teleological argument rests on the analogy between human and divine intelligence and wisdom. Human intelligence is demonstrated by the invention of machines. The universe itself is like a great machine, subdivided into a vast number of smaller machines, which again allow for further subdivisions to an infinite degree of complexity. The ways in which the parts contribute to the whole and the means are adapted to the ends, resemble the work of human designers. The universe, to be sure, is a much greater machine than the machines that humans create. Thus, the Author of Nature, God, the divine designer, has a much higher level of intelligence and wisdom as compared to our human intelligence. This, in short, is Hume's summary of the teleological argument.

Hume criticized this argument in a number of ways. First of all, when we reason from "effect" to "cause," we must be careful not to attribute to the cause any qualities that are beyond those that are manifested in the effect. In the teleological argument, we are reasoning from the effect (the universe) to the cause (God). But we must face the following questions: Is the universe perfect? Is the universe totally good? Since it would be hard to answer in the affirmative, we are not entitled to say that the cause of the universe is a God who is infinitely perfect and good. Furthermore, it is a mistake to make confident judgments about a cause (God) when we have observed only one example of its effect (our universe). Our perspective is very limited. Our belief that our universe is nearly perfect, for example, would be similar to John Doe's belief that his girlfriend is nearly perfect although he has only dated one girl. In both cases, we run into the problem of the limited nature of our experience and point of view. Moreover, even if we think of the universe as a nearly perfect machine, this still does not allow us to make inference about the process by which it came into being. It is possible that a series of lesser "creators," through a process of trial and error, involving a series of mistakes and corrections, brought our universe into being in the way in which we now experience it. Furthermore, thinking of the universe as a machine might not be entirely appropriate. The universe might be more like a living organism than like a machine. These considerations make it difficult to infer that there was one infinitely perfect and benevolent divine designer who brought the universe into being. In these ways, Hume criticized the teleological argument.

Hume also criticized the cosmological argument. This argument, in one of its versions, is based on the view that everything that exists must be the effect of some cause, other than itself. And this cause must be the effect of a previous cause. Since the series of causes cannot go to infinity, we must assume that there is a self caused first cause – God. Hume's objection here is the idea that the universe itself may be "the necessarily existent being."

Hume's criticisms were designed to question the validity of our inferences from the nature of the world to the idea of a God. This means that he was an agnostic. Hume did not imply that he could prove that God did not exist. He simply questioned the classic proofs that were offered.

KANT

Kant, in the philosophy of religion, was famous in two ways. On a purely intellectual plane, he was an agnostic, but on a moral plane, he was a theist. Let us explore his arguments for these perspectives.

Kant's agnosticism was based on his criticism of the ontological argument. He believed, rightly or wrongly, that the teleological and cosmological arguments hinged on the ontological argument. But this argument, according to Kant, was based on an illegitimate philosophical procedure, namely, the attempt to derive "existence" from "essence." What exactly does this mean?

The essence of something is the set of necessary features which constitutes its logical definition. The existence of something is a contingent fact which is illustrated in the world. The classic example of something that has an essence without having an existence, is the unicorn. The unicorn is essentially a horse with one horn but it does not exist. Thus, there is a clear distinction between "essence" and "existence."

According to the ontological argument, however, the essence of God implies God's existence. Kant objects to this assertion by insisting that existence is not a predicate or a characteristic. To understand this contention, let us think of the essence of a car that we might admire. The following features might come to mind: a V8 engine, anti-lock brakes, power steering, etc. Now suppose we add "existence"? This would not add to the concept of the car because existence is not a characteristic of something. This means that, for instance, whereas John's bachelorhood implies John's masculinity, God's essence cannot imply God's existence. Thus, Kant believes that the ontological argument is defective.

For Kant, however, a moral argument may serve to establish the existence of God. For the moral universe to work in an orderly manner, moral virtue should be rewarded and moral vice should be punished. This is real justice. During the course of life, unfortunately, this is not always the case. Good people sometimes suffer while scoundrels prosper. To restore the proper balance in the moral universe, it is necessary for good people to be rewarded and bad people to be punished, at least in the after-life. God alone can guarantee this. Thus, although we can't prove God's existence based on pure reason, our practical reasoning leads us to think of God as a necessary assumption for morality. Thus, Kant set forth a type of moral argument in support of theism.

PALEY

William Paley (1743-1805) was a British philosopher who set forth another version of the teleological argument. His argument may be summarized as follows: If we came across a huge rock in a forest, we might suppose that the rock was always there. On the other hand, if we find a watch, we are not entitled to make a similar assumption because its components provide clear evidence of a complex design. Even a poorly functioning watch displays evidence of careful design. With regard to human beings, the eye, a relatively small part of the body, displays a very complex design. With regard to the world, the various parts of nature are fitted together in a pattern which displays a very complex, comprehensive design. To account for the design in nature, we must conclude that it was designed by a divine designer, namely, God.

This argument by analogy was the most popular pre-Darwinian version of the teleological argument. Darwin's evolutionary theory, with its principle of natural selection, may be seen as a counter-argument to the design argument. In recent years, however, the classic design argument was resurrected in the "intelligent design" movement. Philip Johnson, Michael Behe and William Dembski have written books to restate the design argument in mathematical and scientific terms. On the other hand, evolutionary thinkers have objected to all attempts to revive the teleological argument. Perhaps the most famous recent attack on the design argument is found in Richard Dawkins' The Blind Watchmaker. The book's title, of course, reminds us of Paley's watch analogy. In contrast to Paley, Dawkins believed that time and chance, rather than divine design, can explain the development of life in our universe. Thus, Paley's design argument continues to inspire supporters and detractors.

NEWMAN

John Henry Newman (1801-1890) was a cardinal who contributed a moral argument to the philosophy of religion. Cardinal Newman believed that religious and moral truths are different from mathematical and logical truths. Concrete moral issues are different from abstract logical notions. Nevertheless, our moral conscience is just as reliable as our memory and our logical intelligence. Our moral conscience leads us to feel a sense of responsibility and moral duty. This sense of moral duty cannot be explained simply in terms of loyalty to abstract moral principles, however. We do not feel guilty before an abstract principle. We feel guilt before a Supreme Governor or Judge of the moral universe, namely, God. Thus, the dictates of conscience implies the existence of God, to whom we are answerable for the moral conduct of our lives.

MARX

Karl Marx was a political philosopher, rather than a philosopher of religion. His outlook, however, had a great impact in this field and, consequently, needs to be taken into account.

Marx's one-liner is the following: "Religion is the opiate of the people." By this statement, he meant that religion offers comfort to people who are oppressed by the dominant class in society. This comfort, however, is based on the idea of a better world in the after-life. Thus, according to Marx, religion is frequently used as a tool of the dominant class to keep the working class in an inferior position in society. It is, therefore, an instrument of oppression rather than liberation. This is the basic reason for Marx's atheism.

KIERKEGAARD

Soren Kierkegaard (1813-1855) was a founding father of religious existentialism. Existentialism is the view that there is no fixed universal human essence. The individual must create his or her essence by virtue of making choices. For the existentialist, the will rather than reason is the most important aspect of human personality. To be a human being is to be engaged in making life-defining choices on a continuous basis.

Religion, for the existentialist, is not a search for pure objective truth but a passionate commitment of faith. Kierkegaard believed that there were three stages of life: the aesthetic, the ethical, and the religious. The aesthetic stage is characterized by the pleasures of the senses. The ethical state is based on the idea of moral duty. The religious stage is characterized by faith. A playboy, for instance, is driven by his desire for sensual pleasures and has no moral commitment to any of his lovers. He represents the aesthetic stage. Socrates, for instance, was willing to die for his philosophical beliefs. His sense of moral duty shows that he represents the ethical stage. Abraham, however, was willing to sacrifice his son's life in order to obey God's command. Even though, further in the story, God prevented Abraham from sacrificing his son, his willingness to submit to God's will shows that he represents the religious stage.

For Kierkegaard, religious faith is the highest stage of life. Faith, in his view, however, is not based on reason but on a subjective commitment of the will. Kierkegaard thinks of this commitment as a "leap of faith" which goes beyond objective reasoning and leads to personal salvation.

NIETZSCHE

Nietzsche was a founding father of atheistic existentialism. Like Kierkegaard, he believed that truth is subjective rather than objective. But whereas Kierkegaard was passionately committed to theism, Nietzsche was a passionate atheist.

Nietzsche's famous one-liner was "God is dead." This means that there is no rational plan in the universe and no objective standard for human values. The masses, whose actions are based on the conventional standards of society, lead lives of mediocrity and conformity. Authentic individuals, however, should invent their own subjective values and lead lives of excellence and creativity. Insofar as religion fosters social conformity rather than individual creativity, it does not lead us to the highest values, according to Nietzsche's outlook.

FREUD

Freud (1856-1939) was a psychoanalyst rather than a philosopher. Nevertheless, he formulated a view of religion which was quite influential. Like Marx and Nietzsche, he was one of the most famous atheists in the history of ideas.

For Freud, religion was based on an illusion. Whereas science is based on verifiable facts, religion is based on wishful thinking. The wish for security gives rise to the idea that God is our divine parent. The wish for eternal life gives rise to our belief in a heavenly world. The wish for perfect justice gives rise to the belief in a future utopia on earth. In all of these cases, Freud believed that religious revelations are simply childish illusions which hinder the development of a scientific understanding of the facts of reality.

JAMES

William James (1842-1910) applied the idea of pragmatism to the philosophy of religion. According to the pragmatist, a belief counts as knowledge if it allows us to act successfully in the world, and a proposition is true if it works.

Now the question is how to evaluate theism and atheism from a pragmatic point of view. Agnosticism is ruled out by James because, although it might be great on a purely intellectual level, on a practical level, people will live as if there is or is not a God. Thus, theism or atheism must be chosen in practice.

In making a choice regarding God's existence, James believed that there are good rational arguments on both sides. This sort of question, then, has to be decided on a practical level. We cannot simply suspend judgment, because, in the case of God's existence, our choice involves a momentous and forced decision. Our passions, hopes, and fears are involved. We hope to believe the truth and we fear falling into errors. Should we act on our fear or on our hope? If we embrace atheism and our fear of falling into error, we may miss out on some of the psychological benefits of theism. Thus, James believed that since reasons and facts, by themselves, cannot decide the issue, we have a right to believe in God due to psychological and practical reasons. In short, this expresses James' pragmatic approach to the philosophy of religion.

FLEW

Antony Flew (1923-2010) set forth an agnostic view in the philosophy of religion based on the theory of knowledge that we associate with logical positivism. For the logical positivist, there are two kinds of meaningful propositions, those that are analytic and those that are synthetic. An analytic proposition is always necessarily true because it is based on a logical definition. On the other hand, a synthetic proposition is true if it is based on factual verification. Examples of analytic propositions include the following: Palm Beach widows have at least one dead husband. Bachelors are unmarried males. Examples of synthetic propositions include the following: Palm Beach widows tend to be wealthy. Shaq is over seven feet tall.

How would we classify religious propositions? Examples of these propositions include the following: God exists. God is good. God is love. Are these propositions analytic or synthetic? If the ontological argument is valid, it would imply that "God exists" is an analytic proposition. Since we tend to think of religious propositions as factual statements, rather than mere definitions, however, we think of them as synthetic propositions. As such, Flew, as a logical positivist, wanted to know the ways in which religious propositions could be verified.

Factual statements may be verified by appealing to our sensory experience. By using a tape measure, for instance, we could verify that Shaq is over seven feet tall. If we were to deny this statement, however, we would not automatically be guilty of contradicting ourselves. We could imagine a scenario where Shaq had to get his legs amputated to save his life, for example. Synthetic propositions are verifiable and we can imagine cases where they could be falsified. Analytic propositions can never be falsified because they are always true by definition. We can never imagine a case where we encounter a "married bachelor," for example. On the other hand, synthetic propositions are open to verification or falsification. To imagine that they could be false is to see that they are meaningful.

Can we falsify religious propositions? This was Flew's central question in the philosophy of religion. What would have to happen for us to claim the following? : God does not exist. God is not good. God is not love. If the theistic response is that nothing can ever make these religious propositions false, then unless the theist is prepared to think of them as mere definitions, they are, in fact, meaningless, since they would not qualify as synthetic propositions.

Propositions that are neither true nor false are meaningless, according to Flew's logical positivism. For Flew, a statement like "God is good," is similar to a statement like "Mary's car failed to start due to fate." Both statements can neither be verified nor falsified. This means that both statements are meaningless. This verdict also applied to their negations. In other words, "God does not exist" and "Mary's car did not fail to start due to fate," are also meaningless statements. Hence, from the standpoint of Flew's early work in this field, both theism and atheism were seen as meaningless. Agnosticism appeared to him to be the most reasonable view.

Very late in his philosophical career, Flew reversed his position. He eventually defended a theistic view, but for most of his career he was an ardent supported of agnosticism based on his application of logical positivism.

PLANTINGA

Alvin Plantinga (1932-) used the theory of foundationalism in order to defend theism. A foundationalist believes that knowledge is built on self-evident axioms or requires a base of certainty. Every belief in a system of beliefs, however, does not have to be verified by our sensory experience. Foundational beliefs are exempted from this requirement. Reason recognizes them as necessary assumptions in order for us to have any valid beliefs whatsoever. Foundational beliefs are the axioms of a belief system.

Plantinga used the term "basic belief" to describe a foundational belief. God, for Plantinga, is a basic belief that is in the same epistemological boat, so to speak, as the belief in "other minds." Although we can never verify that "other minds" exist by appealing to the data of our sensory experiences, we must assume that this belief is true in order to have a conversation with anyone. In like manner, although we cannot verify the existence of God by appealing to the data of our sensory perceptions, we must assume that there is a God in order to explain such things as the order and rationality of the universe. God, for this foundationalist, is a basic belief in the theistic system of beliefs. Thus, the belief in God does not depend on other beliefs for its justification, according to Plantinga.

DALY

Mary Daly (1928-2010) was a philosophical supporter of feminism who wanted to reinterpret the traditional symbols of theism. In her view, traditional theism was infected by a male bias.

To think of God as a heavenly Father and Lord, is to think of God in exclusively male terms. Male-oriented power in heaven, however, justifies male domination and manipulation of women on earth. The God of patriarchal societies encourages one-sex symbolism in spiritual matters. This adoration of maleness implies the total subjugation of women.

Does this mean that women should embrace atheism in order to be true to the mission of women's liberation? Daly did not think so. She thought that spirituality is necessary for women to maximize their potentiality. What is needed is a change in religious consciousness and language. We should think of God as Be-ing, or the power of being, which will inspire female becoming. Thus, by going beyond the limited traditional patriarchal idea of God, we open up new possibilities to inspire women with existential courage to be all that they can be.

REVIEW QUESTIONS

1. Explain the difference between theism, agnosticism, and atheism.
2. Contrast the ontological argument with the cosmological argument for theism.
3. Explain the major versions of the moral argument for theism.
4. Explain the teleological argument for theism.
5. Contrast the mystical approach with the practical approach to theism.
6. Compare the prudential and the pragmatic argument for theism.
7. Explain the impact of foundationalism and feminism on the idea of God.
8. Explain the major arguments for agnosticism.
9. Explain the key arguments for atheism.
10. Justify your favorite perspective in the philosophy of religion.

chapter 6

Philosophical Skills and Systems

THE WORLD OF PHILOSOPHIZING

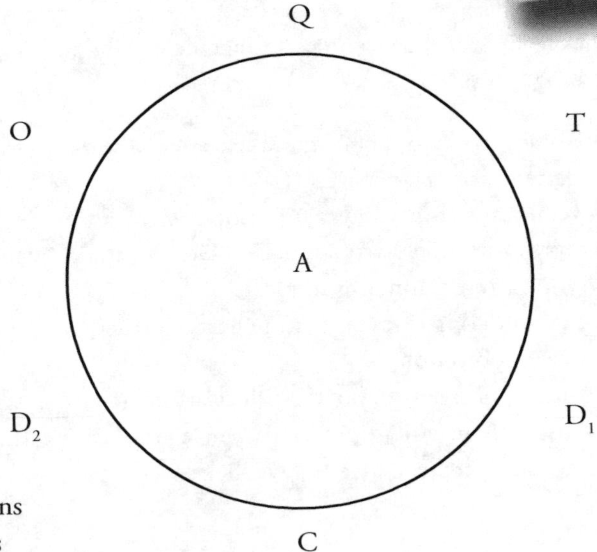

1. Q = Questions
2. T = Theories
3. D_1 = Distinctions
4. C = Connections
5. D_2 = Definitions
6. O = Objections
7. A = Arguments

Philosophers question ideas in order to discover their ultimate assumptions and implications. Ideas which deserve philosophical investigations are those that are central, controversial, and comprehensive. To understand critical ideas, philosophers seek to look at them from a variety of perspectives. By exploring several theories, we avoid, "tunnel vision" which restricts our viewpoints. Philosophers look for distinctions (differences) and connections (similarities) between ideas. Philosophers strive to define ideas with necessary and sufficient criteria. They seek to check previous definitions or arguments by setting forth objections. Answering these objections requires the construction of arguments. Finding good supporting reasons for arguments is perhaps the central activity of philosophical thinking.

General Competencies

A student who wishes to master the essential competencies of a philosopher should focus on developing the following skills:

(1) identifying the basic questions about morality, society, truth, knowledge, and God
(2) exploring a wide range of perspectives
(3) articulating several distinctions and connections between theories
(4) defining concepts with necessary and sufficient criteria, coupled with extensive supporting examples and counter-examples
(5) justifying the rank ordering of criteria, to reflect priorities, with good reasons
(6) answering a range of objections
(7) constructing comprehensive arguments, with clearly stated premises, to justify a position
(8) participating frequently in philosophical dialoguing to clarify, formulate, and appreciate personal, professional, intellectual, and civic beliefs

Special Areas and Applications

AREAS OF CONCERN	WORLDS OF PHILOSOPHY	APPLICATIONS OF SKILLS
1. Morality	Ethics	(A) Sharing recipe of virtues for a Good Life (B) Justifying stance on an ethical issue
2. Society	Political Philosophy	(A) Generating essential criteria for a Good Society (B) Articulating reasons for party preference
3. Reality	Metaphysics	(A) Categorizing general features of reality (B) Explaining acceptance or rejection of "free will" and "immortality"
4. Veracity (Truth) Knowledge	Epistemology	(A) Rank ordering criteria for knowledge (B) Prescribing actions for knowing and learning
5. Divinity	Philosophy of Religion	(A) Creating criteria for the general essence of a possible deity (B) Constructing arguments and counter-arguments for God's existence

REPRESENTATIVE SYSTEMS

One of the skills that we have not paid much attention to is the skill of synthesizing or connecting ideas. Philosophers, throughout the ages, have analyzed, synthesized, and evaluated ideas. To analyze ideas is to break them down into their component parts. To synthesize ideas is to blend them together. To evaluate ideas is to make reasoned value judgments about them.

In the introductory chapter, we focused on analysis by examining procedures for defining concepts – using necessary and sufficient generic criteria along with specific examples and counter-examples. We also touched on evaluation by discussing the need to make judgments based on our reasonable value priorities. To examine the ways in which philosophers practice the art of synthesis, however, we have to explore representative systems of thought. These systems demonstrate the connections between ideas as they relate to "reality," "knowledge," "society," "morality," and "divinity." Systems of beliefs are expressed in the various schools of thought in philosophy. To illustrate some of the major philosophical systems, let us examine the following: Neo-Thomism, Dialectical Materialism, Pragmatism, Positivism, Realism, Personalism, Phenomenology, Existentialism, and Analytic Philosophy.

Neo-Thomism is the belief system that is favored by many thinkers in the world of Roman Catholicism. Pope Leo XIII, in 1879, made Thomism the official view of the Catholic Church. During the twentieth century, philosophers like Etienne Gilson and Jacques Maritain, revived and developed the ideas of St. Thomas Aquinas.

Neo-Thomism begins by assuming that there is an ultimate harmony between faith and reason. This means that religion and philosophy should be complimentary. Some truths are derived from faith only or from reason only. Other truths, however, come from both sources at once. The existence of God, for example, is revealed in Sacred Scriptures and is also derived from natural human reason and experience. St. Thomas Aquinas, we recall, believes that there are five ways to prove God's existence.

Thomistic metaphysics sets forth a series of gradations in Being. Brute matter is at the bottom, minerals, vegetation, animals, humans, angels, and God are included in ascending order. All physical entities, from the level of humans down to the lowest level of matter, consist of both form and matter. God, as universal Spirit, is pure form or perfect actuality. Potentiality, on the other hand, is associated with material entities.

Thomistic ethics and politics blend religious idealism with Aristotelian naturalism. In ethics, virtues like faith, hope, and love are emphasized for attaining eternal happiness; while virtues like wisdom, courage, and temperance are recommended for temporal happiness. In politics, a blend of monarchy, aristocracy, and democracy is put forward as the best system for society.

Dialectical Materialism is the official belief system in the world of communism. It is sometimes called Marxism or Economic Determinism. It is based on distinctive views of reality, truth, society, morality, and religion.

With regard to religion, it is atheistic. Religious ideas like God, the immortal soul, and spiritual values are seen as illusions. Religion is "the opium of the masses." Religion comforts the masses and encourages them not to become liberated from their oppressors. Thus, communism sees religion as a counter-revolutionary force in society. With regard to reality, communism believes that matter alone is real. Religious ideas, like all other ideas, reflect economic interests.

Society is driven by economic forces. Human history is the history of economic classes in conflict. Masters versus slaves, lords versus serfs, factory owners (bourgeoisie) versus factory workers (proletariat) are all various forms of class struggle throughout history. In the future, communism is destined to overthrow the capitalist system, by means of a violent proletarian revolution, and usher in the perfect social system – a classless society.

This outlook on society was shared by Karl Marx, Friedrich Engels, Nicolai Lenin, Josef Stalin, and Mao Tse-tung. Mao, in particular, emphasized the idea that the only valid basis for truth is man's social practice. Ideas are verified through social practices – material productions, class struggles, and scientific experiments. With respect to morality, Mao, the apostle of Marx, believed that the key moral virtues are those that reflect a communist culture – selflessness and hard work. Everything, of course, is predicated on the common ownership of the means of production. Private property is seen as the root of all moral and historical evils.

Pragmatism is a school of thought that originated in the United States of America. The three wise men of pragmatism are Charles Peirce, William James, and John Dewey. This movement has a distinctive outlook on questions relating to reality, knowledge, morality, society, and religion.

Pragmatists tend to be indifferent to questions relating to the ultimate nature of reality. They tend to regard metaphysical questions as inconsequential and focus on the practical consequences of all ideas. If an idea works in practice, it is seen as true. Dewey, the popularizer of pragmatism, characterized his view as instrumentalism or experimentalism. On this view, there are no fixed, eternal, unchanging ideal realities that our ideas must correspond to in order to be true. Ideas are instruments for problem solving. We must adopt an experimental attitude regarding all our beliefs. Those beliefs that produce successful "habits of action" may be seen as true, with respect to a particular place and time.

The pragmatic attitude has important consequences for dealing with views on society, morality, and religion. Democracy tends to be very compatible with their pluralistic outlook and their preference for an open and experimental approach to all social issues. Morality itself, on this view, is social. Moral values are guides to satisfying social needs. We must continuously strive to make the world a better place. The growth in scientific intelligence contributes to the growth of moral intelligence by emphasizing public, objective, and useful ideas for the benefit of humankind. With respect to religion, James believed that it produced positive psychological consequences – earnestness, zest, peace, love, etc. – and therefore should be seen as true.

Whereas James was a theist, Dewey was a religious humanist. He recommended "a common faith," freed from the limits of sect, race, class, etc., that all people could practice. Such a religious faith would aim at inspiring people to pursue the ideal ends of science and democracy.

Positivism, as a school of thought, may refer to classical positivism or logical positivism. Classical positivism came from the ideas of August Comte (1798-1857), the father of sociology. He had distinctive views on religion, morality, knowledge, and reality. Comte believed that God equals Humanity. This sort of religious humanism had the following mantra: Love is the principle. Order is the basis and progress is the aim. Humanitarianism, or altruism, became the highest duty and the greatest blessedness for human beings. In this religion of humanity, ethics, rather than religious dogma, became central.

Comte believed that knowledge evolved in three stages – the theological stage, the metaphysical stage, and the positive stage. In the theological stage, people explain natural phenomena as the results of the workings of spirits or gods. In the metaphysical stage, natural phenomena are explained by impersonal forces called scientific laws. Scientific principles are substituted for polytheistic gods as the ultimate causes for events. In the third and final stage, the positive stage, natural phenomena are explained in terms of experimentally verifiable laws. Human knowledge thus evolves in these stages, according to classical positivism.

Logical positivism was founded by Moritz Schlick in 1924. Philosophers formed a group called, "The Vienna Circle," to develop their perspective on things. They had a unique view on reality, religion, morality, and knowledge.

Their theory of reality revolved around materialism or physicalism. They rejected all beliefs from being considered as knowledge if they violated the principle of verification. According to this principle, all statements are meaningless unless they are true by definition or verifiable in terms of our sensory experiences.

What does this imply for metaphysics, religion, and morality? The logical positivists believed that our beliefs about any non-physical ultimate reality, God and morality are all based on propositions that are, by nature, incapable of being verified. In religion, this leads them to argue for agnosticism. In morality, this outlook is associated with an emotive theory of ethics. Ethics, for the positivists, expresses feelings rather than concepts or facts. Thus, the positivists restricted knowledge to mathematics and the sciences.

There is a major problem with logical positivism, however. Their foundational principle, the principle of verification, cannot be verified. Thus, it seems to undermine itself. Nevertheless, even though most philosophers would not classify themselves as logical positivists, a milder form of empiricism is still attractive to many thinkers.

Realism is a school of thought that stands in contrast with idealism. Realists challenge the notion that reality depends on the human mind. Berkeley's famous statement, "To be is to be perceived," is seen as a fundamental error, according to this view. Realists believe that reality is independent of the process of knowing. Knowledge is about entities that are objectively real and not merely about subjective constructs of the mind.

Realists tend to focus on the process of analysis. They frown on explanations that focus on the purpose of things. They believe that explanations of reality must be made in terms of the basic parts revealed in reductionist analysis.

PERSONALISM

Personalism is the view that personality is the key to reality and value. Ultimate reality bears the marks of personality. Nothing can be understood without an appeal to personality. Meaning exists only for persons. Values exist only for persons. Moral values and artistic values make no sense without persons.

Persons alone possess infinite intrinsic value. Mere objects have instrumental value or exchange value. Persons, however, are above all price owing to their ultimate intrinsic value. The Cosmic Mind, the World-Ground, or God is the Supreme Person and imparts value to the objects in the universe. All particular objects and persons are united by the Cosmic Person – God. Personality is the only entity that can reconcile the metaphysical polarities, namely, unity, and diversity, permanence and change. A person is a complex unity, having a stable identity yet capable of changing. Thus, personality is the glue that holds everything together, according to personalism.

PHENOMENOLOGY

Phenomenology was founded by Edmund Husserl (1859-1938) and developed by Max Scheler (1874-1928). It is based on the idea that the goal of philosophy is to describe the data of human consciousness in an unbiased way, in order to find the essential structures of diverse phenomena. A careful analysis of consciousness, without any scientific or metaphysical theories, is expected to reveal the essence of a wide range of phenomena. A phenomenology of consciousness explores the life-world of human beings by way of the essences disclosed within experience.

EXISTENTIALISM

Existentialism was greatly impacted by phenomenology. Both schools of thought focus their attention on the nature of human consciousness. Existentialism, however, comes in theistic and atheistic categories. Kierkegaard is seen as the founding father of religious existentialism, while Nietzsche is seen as the founder of atheistic existentialists.

All existentialists focus on the primacy of the will, rather than the intellect, in making life-defining choices. They believe that human existence is not rational but filled with powerful feelings of anxiety, abandonment, and despair. Religious existentialists believe in ultimate salvation by a commitment of the will to God. Secular existentialists believe that an authentic life must continuously affirm the absolute freedom of the will to pursue projects of self creation.

Existentialists tend to be critical of the claim that science provides us with universal objective truth about the human condition. For them, truth resides in subjectivity. The individual subject must create his or her unique truth by the choices that are made in life, with regard to the person one is in the process of becoming.

ANALYTIC PHILOSOPHY

Analytic philosophy has many names: Linguistic Analysis, Logical Analysis, Ordinary Language Philosophy, Oxford Philosophy, and Cambridge School of Analysis. What these names have in common is the tendency to see analysis as the primary job for philosophers.

Analytic philosophy does not search for ultimate metaphysical truth. It searches for the logical clarification of ideas through rigorous analysis of the language and concepts we use to make sense of the world. Famous analytic philosophers include G.E. Moore, Bertrand Russell, Ludwig Wittgenstein, John Wisdom, Gilbert Ryle, and John Austin. It started in Britain but many contemporary American philosophers belong to this school of thought. Many analytic philosophers think of philosophy as an activity rather than a system of beliefs. Clarifying the logical geography of our ideas is their chief contribution to the field.

chapter 7

Revisiting Philosophical Worlds

PHILOSOPHICAL WORLDS

There are several things to do in order to develop a comprehensive personal, institutional, and professional philosophy. The first thing to do is remind ourselves of the belief systems that are reflected in the philosophical schools of thought throughout history. The second thing to do is review the theories of each area of academic philosophy. The third thing is to use the analytical technique of carving out distinctions in order to construct a conceptual map of each philosophical world. The fourth thing is to attempt to answer the key questions in each world of philosophy. The fifth thing to do is to connect the answers in each area of academic philosophy to create a personal system of beliefs. The sixth and final thing to do, when relevant, is to explore institutional and professional beliefs in a systematic manner.

The best way to accomplish these lofty goals is to look at the "big picture" and answer key questions. The "big picture" may be constructed by using essential distinctions to view the logical geography of each world of philosophy. We will look at the ethical world, the political world, the metaphysical world, and the world of religion. Finally, we will examine the world of education and see the place of philosophy in the community of academic disciplines.

The Ethical World

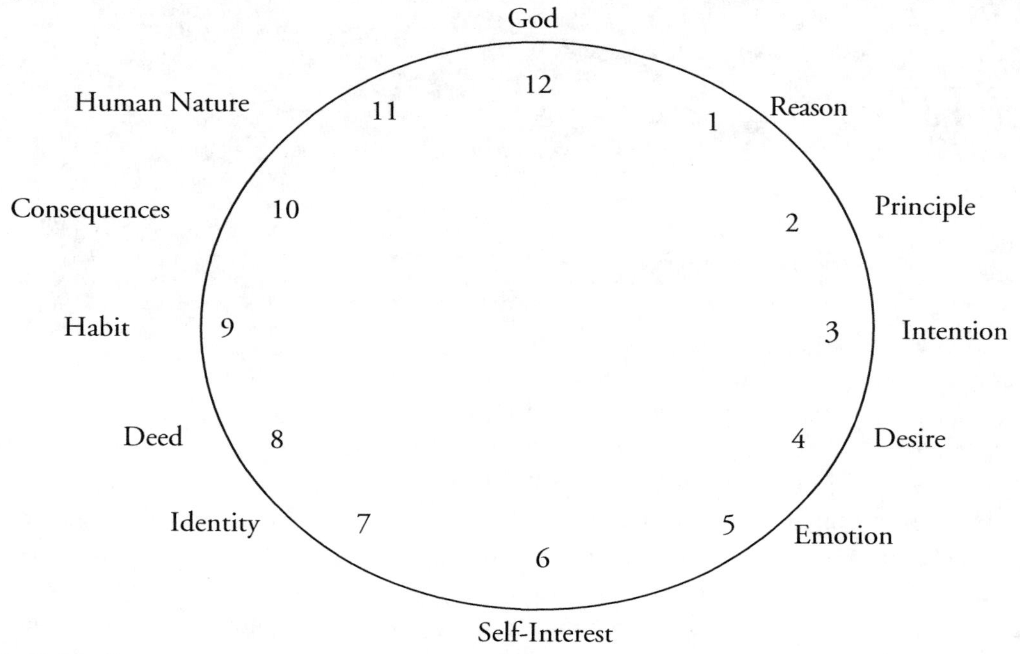

Rationale

The idea behind this ethical model is to use the metaphor of a clock to see what makes us "tick," so to speak, in a moral sense.

Questions

1. What are the key virtues for a Good Life?
2. What is the best way to think of the relationship between duty, happiness, and pleasure?
3. What are our major duties in life?
4. Is morality based on a universal, cultural, or individual standard?
5. What makes something right or wrong?
6. What are the most important moral issues that we face today?
7. What can we do to improve the quality of life, for ourselves and others, on a personal, institutional, and professional level?

The Political World

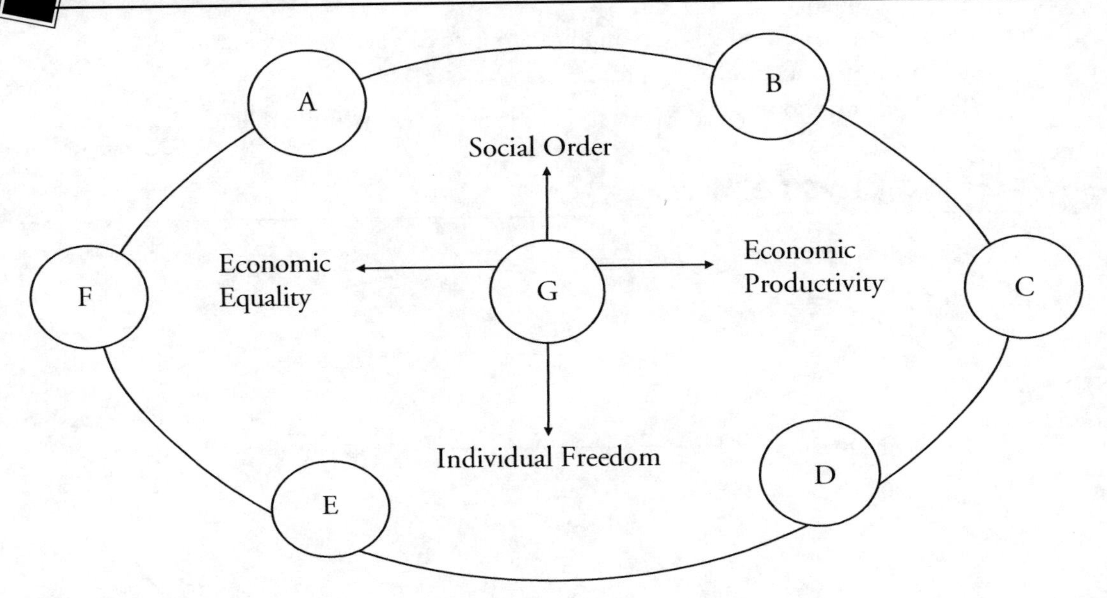

Rationale

The idea behind the political model, is to use the dominant social and economic values in order to notice the relationships between the major political ideologies.

Major Ideologies

(A) communism
(B) fascism
(C) capitalism
(D) libertarianism
(E) liberalism
(F) socialism
(G) centrism

Questions

1. What is the best way to think of the relationship between social order and individual freedom?
2. Should our society have more social order or more individual freedom?
3. Should we have more or less censorship? Why?

4. What is the best way to think of the relationship between economic productivity and economic equality?
5. Should society promote more economic productivity or more economic equality?
6. Should we favor a flat tax or a progressive tax?
7. How does your political party reflect your social and economic values?

The Metaphysical World

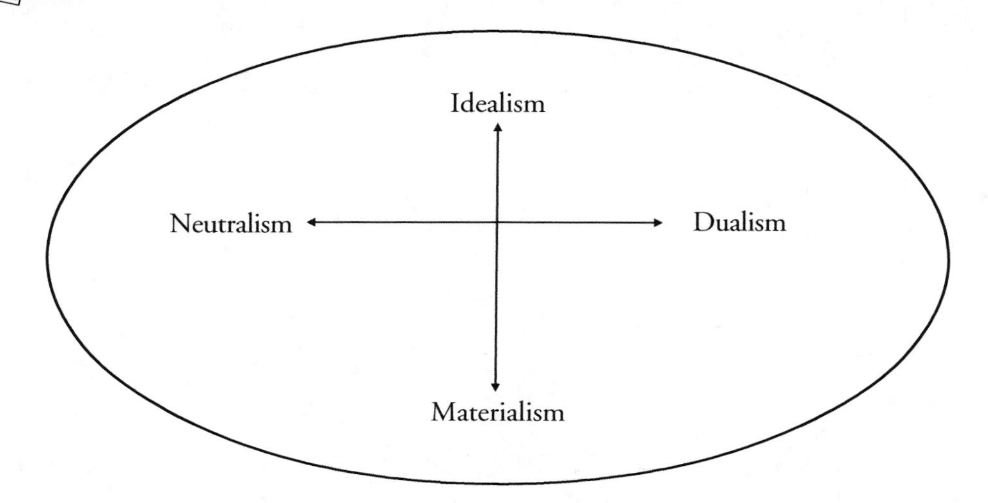

Rationale

The idea behind this metaphysical model is to contrast the major theories in the field.

Distinctions

1) MIND – BODY
2) FREE WILL – DETERMINISM
3) UNIVERSALS – PARTICULARS
4) PERMANENCE – CHANGE
5) UNITY – DIVERSITY

Questions

1. Is there a non-physical mind or an immortal soul?
2. Is there a free will?
3. Are human beings programmed to act by external forces?
4. Are universal concepts more real than particular things?
5. Is a universal concept of Beauty more real than a particular individual like "Miss America"?
6. Is the ultimate reality something permanent or something that is constantly changing?
7. Is unity more real than diversity?

The Epistemological World

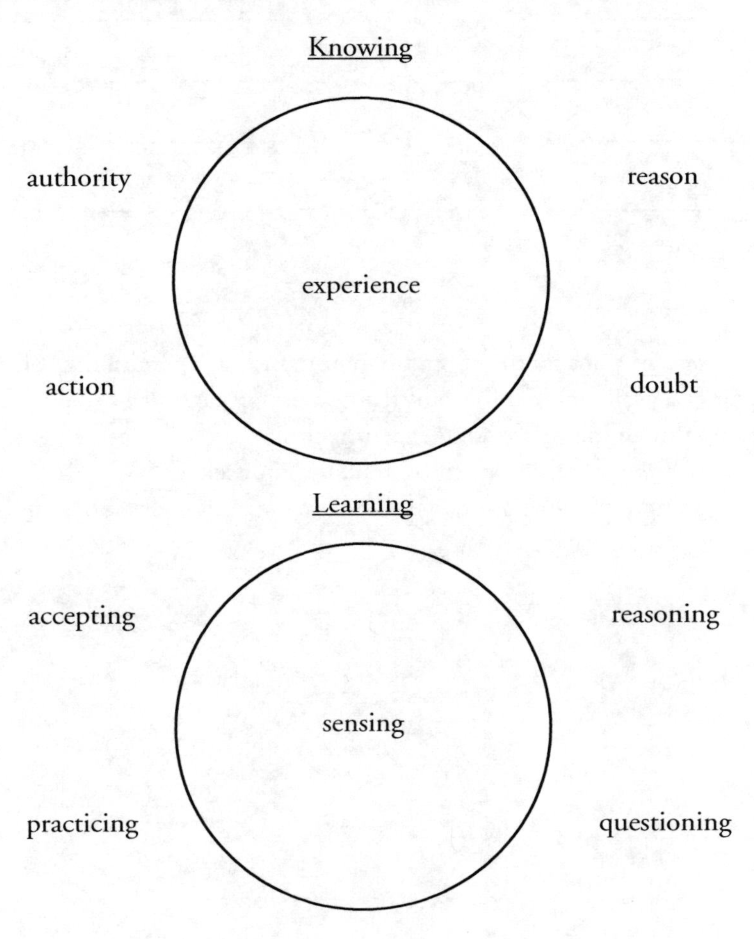

Rationale

The purpose of these conceptual maps is to illustrate the contrasting ways our beliefs may be justified with regard to knowing and learning. We should note that whereas "truth" is a necessary criterion for knowing, it is not a necessary feature of the concept of learning. It would be a contradiction to claim to have knowledge of a proposition that is false. It would not be a contradiction, however, to claim to learn about something that is false. Nevertheless, there is a strong connection between knowing and learning. This is the reason for the maps.

Justifying Beliefs

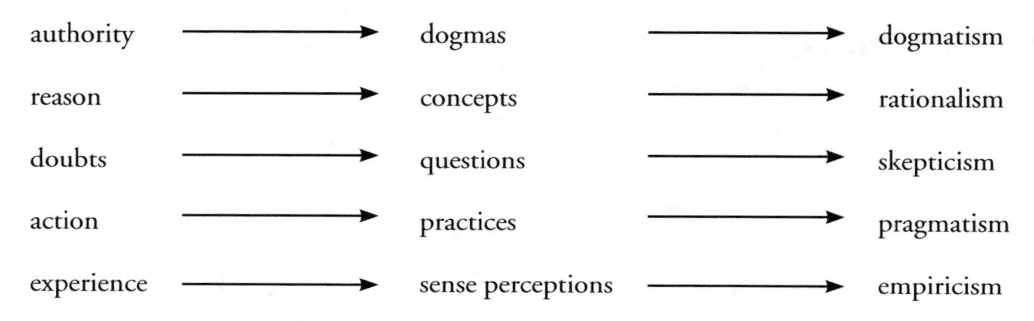

Questions

1. Is accepting traditional authority more important than questioning beliefs?
2. Is thinking logically more important than observing carefully?
3. Is reasoning more important than experimenting?
4. What is the best rank order for the criteria for knowledge?
5. How are your criteria for knowledge related to your strategies for learning?

The World of Religion

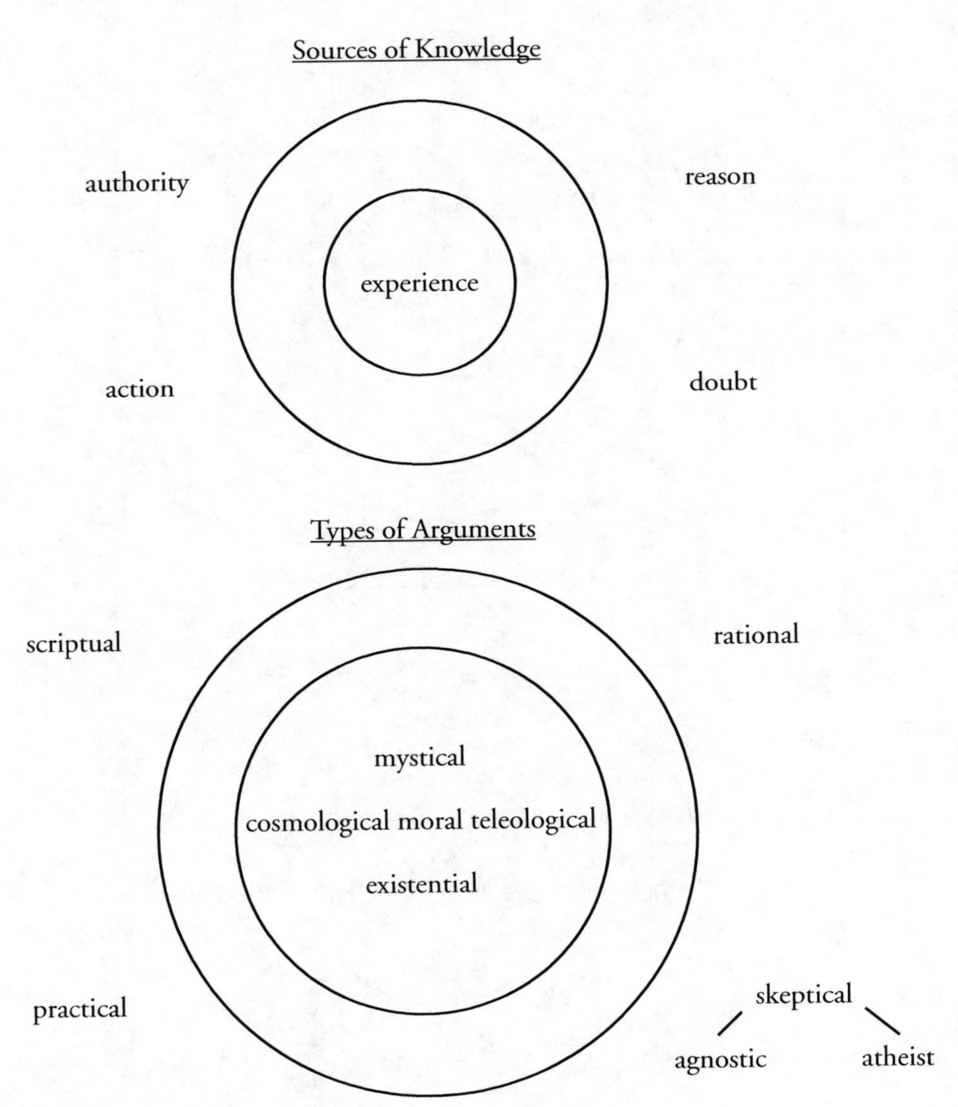

Rationale

The purpose of the above illustration is to show the connections between the sources of knowledge and the types of arguments in the philosophy of religion.

Universal Experiences and Concepts

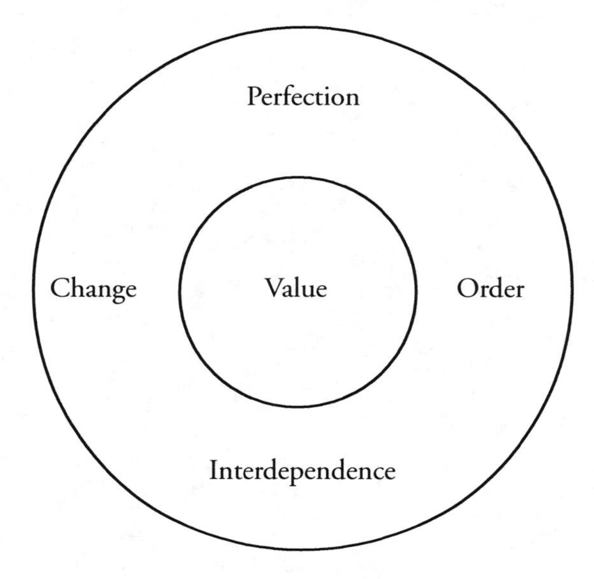

Particular Religious Attitudes

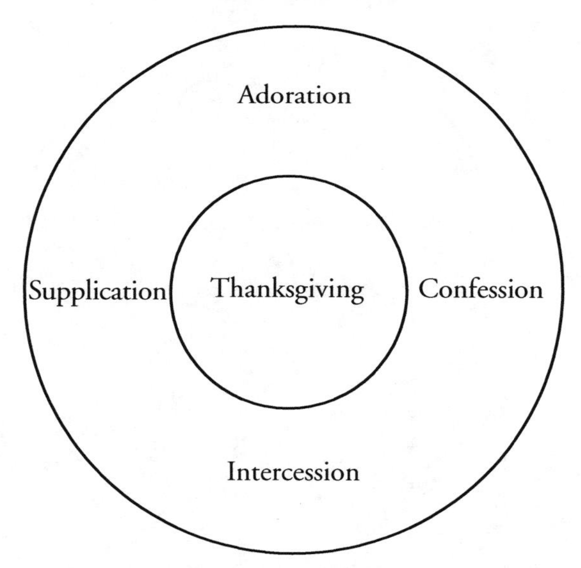

Rationale

The purpose of the above maps is to connect universal experiences and concepts with particular religious attitudes. The specific attitude of adoration, for example, is associated with the generic idea of the perfection of the deity. The particular attitude of thanksgiving is related to the universal concept of value, etc.

Questions

1. What are the bases for the different versions of theism?
2. What are the bases for agnosticism?
3. What are the reasons for the different types of atheism?
4. What are the reasons for your perspective?

THE PLACE OF PHILOSOPHY IN THE ACADEMIC AND PROFESSIONAL WORLDS

We have explored some of the major worlds within the world of philosophy. At this juncture, it is time to examine the place of philosophy in the academic and professional universe. How is philosophy similar to other disciplines? How is philosophy a unique area of study? To examine these questions, we have to try to understand the logical geography of all of the disciplines.

Each discipline, or area of inquiry, involves a special kind of meaning. Educational philosopher Philip Phenix, in Realms of Meaning, develops the idea that there are three basic types of meaning in the disciplines – Form, Fact, and Norm. Formal meanings involve mathematical, philosophical, linguistic, and artistic patterns. Factual meanings involve scientific, historical, and personal data or processes. Normative meanings involve ethical or religious values, desires, or purposes. Each discipline can be recognized by the distinctive type of meaning it engenders.

Each discipline, or domain of inquiry, also involves a unique way of learning. Educational psychologist David Kolb, in Experiential Learning, develops the view that there are four styles of learning – concrete experience, reflective observation, abstract conceptualization, and active experimentation. Although the disciplines use all of the styles of learning, there is a dominant tendency in each academic and professional discipline. If we connect the types of meaning with the styles of learning, we will see the structure of meaningful learning in the academic and professional world.

Let us focus on the types of meaning and the styles of learning in greater detail. Formal meanings deal with patterns. These mental patterns show us the ways in which possibilities may be designed. Forms deal with the realm of logical or artistic possibilities. They show us "what might be." Factual meanings deal with material processes. Facts deal with scientific, historical, or personal data. They show us "what is" or "what was" the case. Moral meanings deal with normative values. They deal with religious visions or ethical purposes. They show us what people believe "ought to be." Learning based on concrete experience emphasizes special perceptions. Learning based on reflective observation emphasizes integral perspectives.

Learning based on abstract conceptualization emphasizes general principles. Learning based on active experimentation emphasizes effectual practices.

The types of meaning may be summarized in the following way:

Formal Mental Patterns → Designs

Factual Material Processes → Data

Functional Moral Purposes → Desires

The styles of learning may be illustrated in the following conceptual map:

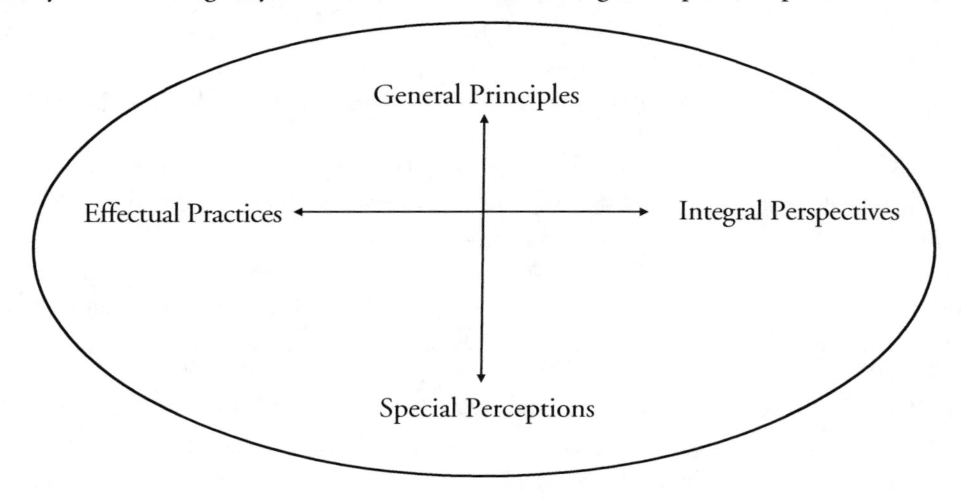

Blending the types of meaning with the styles of learning allows us to set forth the following matrix of academic disciplines and professional careers:

	Formal Patterns	**Factual Processes**	**Moral Purposes**
General Principles (abstractions)	Math/Logic Languages	Natural Sciences Social Sciences	Meta-Ethics Social-Ethics
Integral Perspectives (interpretations)	Philosophy	History	Religion
Special Perceptions (sensations)	Literature Theater Art/Music Dance	Personal Knowledge	Personal Ethics
Professional Practices (applications)	Actuary Journalist Actor Singer	Engineer Doctor Librarian Counselor	Lawyer Social Worker Clergyman Teacher

This matrix of meaningful learning shows the place of philosophy in the academic and professional world. Philosophy deals with integral perspectives in interpreting formal patterns of meaning. Whereas history deals with integrating factual data with respect to time, and religion deals with integrating moral desires with respect to ultimate values, philosophy deals with integrating patterns of ideas with respect to concepts. A knowledge of the world's history, as well as the world's religions, is therefore a valuable resource for the philosopher from the standpoint of understanding and creating integrative perspectives or world-views.

From the standpoint of examining formal patterns, other disciplines also contribute to philosophical competence. Mathematics, for example, the favorite discipline of rationalistic philosophers, helps us to develop skills in working with the general principles of abstract patterns of thought. Literature and the other artistic disciplines allow us to appreciate patterns of meaning by way of sensitive perceptions of significant forms. Great philosophers cultivate the virtues of logical consistency and aesthetic sensitivity.

Does this mean that the professional disciplines have nothing to contribute to, or learn from, philosophy? This might seem to be the case if we restrict ourselves to examining two-dimensional conceptual maps. If we employ a three-dimensional map, however, the relevance of philosophy to every discipline should be more easily discerned. The justification for doing this is that formal, factual, and moral meanings, while different, are not totally exclusive. Factual disciplines, for instance, require formal competence. A good scientist, for example, is well advised to study mathematics. A similar thing can be said for the styles of learning. Special sensations, integral interpretations, abstract conceptualizations and practical applications tend to reinforce one another. General theoretical reflections bear fruit in special practical applications. This is why general education and special training should go hand in hand.

The specialized professional disciplines can contribute to, and learn from, philosophy. Philosophers engage in the analysis, synthesis, and evaluation of patterns of meaning. To search for integrated understanding of the basic ideas in any profession requires a philosophical journey. Law, medicine, and education, for examples, generate very interesting materials for philosophical reflection. Journalism, business, and counseling, for instances, have also contributed to the growing body of literature in the field of ethics. Thus, we can maintain that philosophy is not just an academic discipline, but a dimension of understanding in our professional and personal lives.

Let us summarize these reflections with the following final, three-dimensional, illustration:

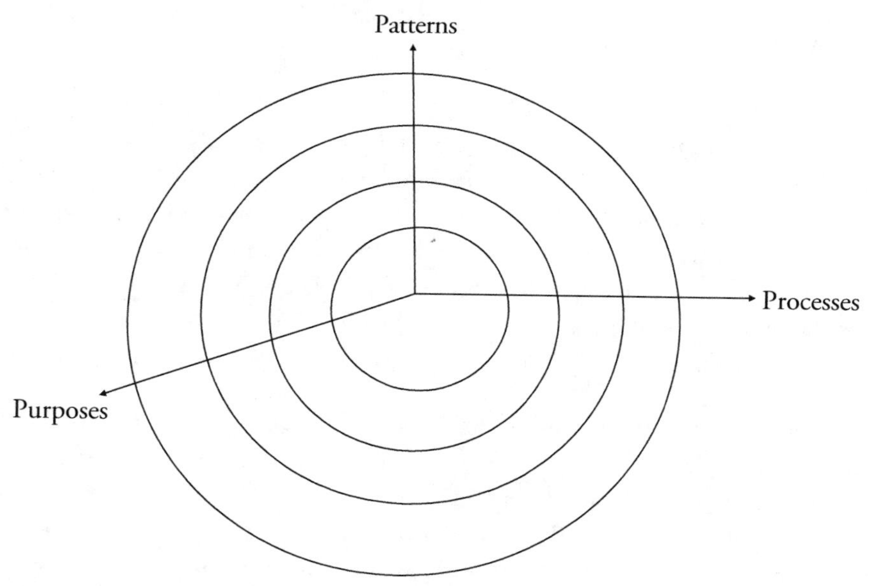

A well-educated person needs the breadth of factual learning about processes, the depth of moral learning about ultimate purposes, and the height of philosophical learning about patterns of meaning. Learning to see patterns of criteria in definitions, patterns of reasons in arguments, and patterns of distinctions and connections in concepts, is learning to philosophize. Philosophy is the record of the ways in which people have tried, in a systematic way, to interpret their experiences. Philosophizing is an exciting, active, and continuous attempt, on a personal and social level, to interpret the many worlds of meaning in which we are privileged to participate.